W9-BXD-162

THE
CIVIL WAR

THE
CIVIL WAR

Jonathan Sutherland & Diane Canwell

CHARTWELL
BOOKS, INC.

This edition published in 2010 by
CHARTWELL BOOKS, INC.
A division of BOOK SALES, INC.
276 Fifth Avenue Suite 206
New York, NY 10001
USA

ISBN-13: 978-0-7858-2705-4
ISBN-10: 0-7858-2705-6

Printed in China

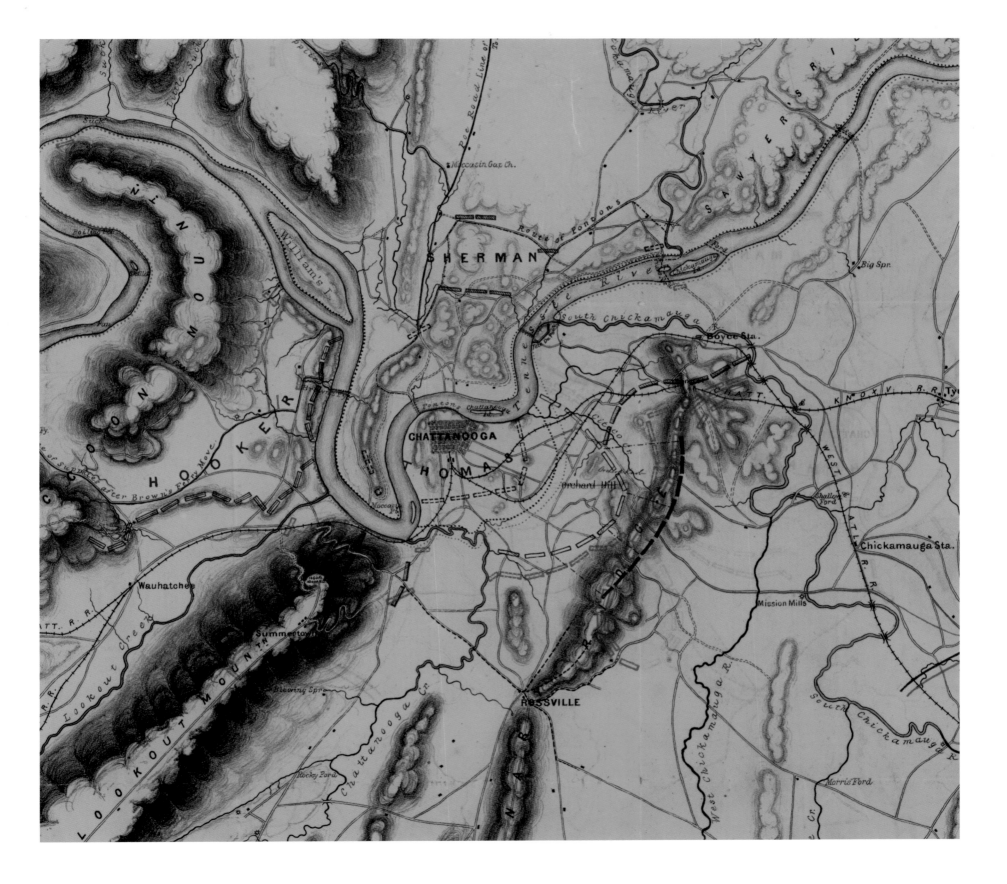

CONTENTS

Departure of the 7th Regiment, New York State Militia, 19 April 1861
George Hayward (c.1800–72).
Graphite pencil, transparent & opaque watercolour on paper.
Museum of Fine Arts, Boston, Massachusetts.

INTRODUCTION

Dependent on the labour of slaves, who represented the great majority of the American black population, the great Southern plantations were both homes and sources of income for a white elite.

For many years after the American Civil War (1861–1865), Northerners would refer to it as the War of the Rebellion. It had been the second conflict in less than a century, the first, the American Revolution (the War of American Independence), having resulted in the Declaration of Independence in 1776 and the expulsion of the British. Many saw the conflict as something more than a popular uprising against an occupying force, regarding it as an event of far-reaching consequence to America and to the world at large. On that occasion, Europe had played a direct role; the British on the one hand, supported by loyalists against the insurgents and their allies, and on the other, America, supported by France and Spain.

Contrary to popular belief, the American Civil War, initially at least, did not arise out of the slave question – its roots lay deeper than that. Southern historians called it 'the war between the states', in that the South saw it as a consequence of the North's resistance to its right to withdraw from the Union, each state seeing itself as sovereign though in confederation with its neighbours.

This was not the first time the Union had been under threat; since 1820 the South had become more and more alarmed by developments within the United States. The North had grown more populous and wealthy, its economy based not on agriculture but on proliferating industry. The South began to see its power slipping away, and its position within the Union beginning to erode. With their distinctive identity and shared past, the Southern states began to see the inevitability of an independent future.

While the Old South did have a distinctive identity of its own, it was not, as many imagined, a huge cotton plantation teeming with slaves controlled by overseers. Slavery was not only endemic in the South, it was also a blight on the lives of the slaves themselves, and a time bomb ready to explode. While the black population of the North was insignificant, in the South it outnumbered its white masters by more than half.

Even as the influence of the South began to wane, tariffs failed to lighten the burden on Southern agriculture. At every turn, Federal policies seemed to favour the North: the South produced vast wealth for the Union, but received very little in return. These grievances were similar to those heard in the 13 colonies in the American Revolution, when 'no taxation without representation' was the call. The South was beginning to perceive itself as little more than an exploited colony.

South Carolina threatened to secede from the Union as early as 1832, at about the same time as militant abolitionists were beginning to gather strength in the North. The abolitionists claimed slavery to be in direct contradiction to the Declaration of Independence in which all men were to be considered equal. In short, the militants believed that slavery and democracy were totally incompatible with one another.

Ten years earlier, slavery had not featured largely in national debates, but with the Mexican War over and huge new territories opening up for settlement, the question of slavery was now very much on the agenda. A compromise was made in 1850, which called only a temporary halt to the debate and the inevitable conflict that would ensue.

The two key issues that would propel the United States into war had not been resolved, despite nearly 50 years of negotiations. First was the issue of secession – the right of a state to leave the Union if it so wished. The second was the unresolved

ABOVE LEFT: A trader in slaves, in Alexandria, Virginia.

ABOVE: The pens where the slaves where kept while they waited to be sold.

INTRODUCTION

question of extending slavery into the new territories. In fact, the spark that would ignite the conflict was the election of Abraham Lincoln in November 1860, and his implacable opposition to the extension of slavery into the new territories.

Extremists on both sides were unwilling to compromise on either issue, and peaceful resolution was now impossible. It would be South Carolina, which had threatened secession 30 years earlier, that would force the issue. On 20 December 1860, at a convention in Charleston, the state adopted an Ordnance of Secession. It repealed its 1788 ratification of the Constitution and proclaimed the new act effective from 24 December 1860.

Hostilities did not begin until the following April: on 12 April 1861 rebel forces opened fire on the Federal-held Fort Sumter in Charleston harbour. The war would officially last for just over four years.

As North and South divided and plunged into war, comrades-in-arms who had known one another from their days at the U.S. Military Academy at West Point went their separate ways. For both officers and rank and file alike, the simple choice was to rally to the flag of their state, regardless of their views of the political situation. Others aligned themselves to their chosen political or philosophical belief, much to the disgust of their families: the American Civil War, like all internal conflicts, truly pitted brother against brother.

In a war that would see massed muskets and terrifying artillery bombardment, casualties were bound to be high. A dense line of men firing at one another at a ruinous distance was a test of nerve. As men fell up and down the line, depleting the firepower and resolve of the regiment, officers put themselves at extreme risk to convince their men to stand firm. Regimental and company officers had only a 15 per cent chance of being killed or wounded, while brigade, divisional and corps commanders were 50 per cent more likely to be hit – simply because they were expected to lead from the front.

The key military figures of the American Civil War were drawn from the tiny pre-war standing army. These men, the majority of whom had passed through West Point, had

THE CIVIL WAR

traditions, realized that, faced by the Union army and navy, it would be hopelessly outnumbered right from the start. On the other hand, the South was blessed with the boldest and most competent commanders. Robert E. Lee and Thomas 'Stonewall' Jackson led the line, taking the initiative and outwitting Union commanders with far greater forces at their disposal. The South had the unenviable task of defending 4,000

LEFT: **The Shackle Broken ...** *Lithograph illustrating Robert B. Elliott's famous speech in favour of the Civil Rights Act, delivered by the House of Representives in 1874.*

BELOW LEFT: Ulysses S. Grant.

BELOW CENTRE: A black soldier.

BELOW: Robert E. Lee.

cut their teeth in earlier clashes, either against the Mexicans or against Native Americans on the frontiers. Men who had graduated bottom of their classes, such as the Confederate John Bell Hood, destined in peacetime to become a quartermaster in some quiet backwater, were catapulted into leading whole armies during the war.

The South, despite its strong military

The First Reading of the Emancipation Proclamation
Francis Bicknell Carpenter (1830–1900).
Oil on canvas.
Library of Congress, Washington, D.C.

INTRODUCTION

RIGHT: Thomas 'Stonewall' Jackson.

BELOW: Philip H. Sheridan.

BELOW RIGHT: William T. Sherman.

miles (6440km) of front against the Union and for the most part chose to do so by taking the offensive and fighting its war in the North's own back yard.

When, eventually, truly competent, visionary and ruthless commanders emerged from the ranks of the Union army, they were able to weald its immense potential power with some precision. Ulysses S. Grant (a future president), William T. Sherman and Philip Sheridan were prime examples of such men, determined to achieve ultimate victory and willing to bring total and destructive war to the South.

There were 1,800 or more engagements between the North and South over the four-year period, and half of these would be classed as all-out battles. With a few notable exceptions, the Confederates invariably inflicted heavier losses on the North, but manpower was always going to be a problem for the South, in that it adamantly refused to officially sanction the recruitment of black soldiers. Despite this, thousands did serve in the ranks of the Confederate armies, and only when it was too late did the South finally concede that it desperately needed black manpower. The North, tentatively at first, recognized the worth of this vast pool of potential soldiers, and against direct orders, black regiments were formed in Kansas and later in the Carolinas. After

THE CIVIL WAR

Emancipation, slowly at first but quickly gathering pace, the Union army began to recruit black troops and over 180,000 would later serve, providing the rank and file of over 100 infantry regiments alone.

Ultimately, the North was to adopt the so-called Anaconda Strategy – the slow, deliberate strangulation of the South. The blockade and eventual capture of Southern coastal cities and the deep, penetrating and destructive forays into the heartland of the South began to take effect.

By November 1864 Grant's armies had failed to penetrate Lee's rings of defence around the Confederate capital of Richmond, and it looked as though the war would drag on and that Lincoln would not be re-elected. But complete Southern collapse was closer than the Confederates dared to admit or even the Unionists could have guessed in all their wildest dreams.

INTRODUCTION

THE CIVIL WAR

Black Troops of the 54th Massachusetts Regiment during the Assault of Fort Wagner, South Carolina, 18 July 1863
Colour lithograph, American School. Private collection.

OPPOSITE and LEFT: Civil War re-enactments.

INTRODUCTION

RIGHT: The White House of the Confederacy, Richmond, Virginia, was the Civil War residence of the Confederate President Jefferson Davis.

OPPOSITE RIGHT ABOVE: The ruins of the Richmond State Arsenal and a bridge of the Richmond & Petersburg Railroad during the Civil War.

OPPOSITE RIGHT: Appomattox Courthouse, Virginia, where General Lee finally surrendered to General Grant in April 1865.

THE CIVIL WAR

The capital finally fell and without it, like many Confederate cities, all hopes for the South lay in ruins. With Union armies converging on the ragtag remnants of his force, Lee had no option but to surrender at Appomattox Courthouse in April 1865, though by then most of the Confederate troops had been imprisoned in Union camps.

The world's largest and most costly civil war had finally come to an end and all that remained of the conflict would be decades of recriminations.

RIGHT: Statue commemorating the Civil War at Lexington, Massachusetts.

OPPOSITE: Hollywood Cemetery, Richmond, Virginia, overlooking the James river, was built as a memorial to the 18,000 or more enlisted men of the Confederate army who lost their lives during the Civil War. Many Union soldiers were also buried here.

CHAPTER ONE

DIXIE, THE OLD SOUTH

The first slaves were brought to Virginia a year before the *Mayflower* arrived in Massachusetts Bay in 1619. However, slavery was already well established in the New World, having been introduced by Portuguese and Spanish colonizers, who used large numbers of the indigenous people as slaves.

Large-scale importation of slaves did not begin until the late-17th century, however, and by the time the 13 colonies had risen up in the American Revolution, slavery was permitted by law. After the revolution, the Northern states, principally Delaware, Massachusetts, New York, New Jersey and Pennsylvania, gradually ended slavery, but the question arises as to why it persisted in the Southern states, when it had become all but extinct in the North. In Virginia and Maryland the key cash crop had been tobacco, but by the end of the 18th century tobacco was no longer as profitable as it once had been. The replacement crop was cotton, rather than wheat, in that it was more suited to the use of slave labour and rather more profitable than wheat.

New manufacturing processes in England had speeded up and reduced the costs of making cotton thread and textiles, which meant an enormous increase in demand for the raw material. There was a problem in that the type of cotton that could be grown in the American South was not easy to handle, it being difficult to separate the cotton threads from the seeds. Eli Whitney produced a working cotton gin in 1794, solving this problem, and from then on cotton farming spread across the Mississippi, the Appalachian Mountains and on to Texas, taking slavery with it. Slaves were also used to tend tobacco crops, rice

SLAVERY AS IT EXISTS IN AMERICA.

SLAVERY AS IT EXISTS IN ENGLAND.

American Civil War, nearly 30 years into the future, it is unlikely that slavery would have died a natural death in the South.

Contrary to most views of the South at this time, the vast majority of whites did not own slaves, and there were only around 25 per cent who did or who were linked directly to slave-owning families. By 1850 around half of these owned less than five slaves, and only one per cent owned more than 100. At the height of the slave-owning period, only four or five slave-owners owned 1,000 slaves, while an average-sized plantation needed no more than 20 or 30 to work cotton, rice or sugar crops. Most slaves did not work on plantations; rather they fulfilled the role of hired hands on Southern farms, working alongside their owners in the fields. In larger plantations, and in cities, there were considerable numbers of highly skilled slaves; these built houses, made casks, laid railroads, drove trains and virtually ran Richmond's tobacco manufacturing industry.

To buy a slave was to make a considerable investment, because once owned, a slave needed to be fed and looked after, even if there was no work. Slave-owners would hire out their slaves, perhaps for $100 a year, having cost the owner between $1,500 and $2,000 to buy. Most of the slaves who constructed the railroads and worked in the tobacco factories in Richmond had been hired out by plantation-owners.

A child born into slavery could be worth as little as $100, but as it reached maturity, its value to the slave-owner would increase. There was a flourishing trade in slaves from Virginia and Maryland, and these were sold to newer states in the Deep South. In fact, after 1808, when further importation of slaves was outlawed, the internal slave trade became a vital part of the system to provide new slaves where they were needed most. In the vast majority of cases mothers were not subjected to the trauma of having their children torn away from them and sold, they were nearly always sold together. Likewise, couples were rarely separated.

The legal position of slaves was,

fields and, in Louisiana, sugar canes. By 1830 the South regarded slavery as an economic necessity.

Elsewhere in the New World slavery was dying out, partly due to economics and partly for ethical reasons. Without the

OPPOSITE: Savannah Cotton Exchange during the Civil War, Savannah, Georgia.

LEFT: **Slavery as it Exists in America**
A cartoon defending slavery.

DIXIE, THE OLD SOUTH

BELOW: A Methodist anti-slavery meeting.

perhaps, the most confusing aspect of the 'peculiar institution', as the Southerners put it. On the one hand slaves were considered chattels, like a chair or a horse – on the other hand, they had responsibility for their own actions, and could be tried in court for any crime they may have committed. In Georgia, for example, the conviction of a slave for murder was quashed at an appeal court hearing on the grounds that the owner had not paid for a defence attorney for his slave.

It is clear that slaves were recognized as human beings in Southern law. In Mississippi in 1821, a white man murdered a slave and his defence was based on the assumption that killing a slave could not be murder. The white judge was having none of this and told the defendant: '[The slave] is still a human being and possesses all those rights, of which he is not deprived by the positive provisions of the law. By the provisions of our law, a slave may commit murder, and be punished by death. Is not the slave a reasonable creature, is he not a human being, [and since] even the killing of a lunatic, an idiot or even a child unborn, is murder, as much as the killing of a philosopher, has not the slave as much reason as a lunatic, an idiot, or an unborn child?' The judge thought the answer was yes and sentenced the murderer to death.

The South wrestled with the paradox of owning another human being, while creating laws to protect the enslaved. Legal protection grew, not least in the case of proving actual ownership, the law presuming that a black person was a slave unless they had documents to prove to the contrary. In practice, this meant that unscrupulous individuals could make forays into non-slave states, snatch black people and present them as slaves in the South. By 1850 the slave population stood at 3.2 million. Each year, however, thousands were freed, many of mixed race, being the offspring of slaves and their former masters.

Slaves could also use the law to obtain their freedom, and could purchase themselves if they were able to save enough money. Usually, when this happened, the former slave was required to leave the state, there being no wish to have large numbers of freed slaves on the loose, that could band together and engineer a revolt. Only six per cent of the black population of the South were freed men and even they were held in comparative poverty by a restrictive mix of custom and law.

By 1860 there were 4 million slaves in the South and just 250,000 freed men. In practice, while laws existed to protect slaves from being punished too harshly by their masters, there was no one to actually police the law. Conditions were therefore variable: wealthier plantation owners were able to provide more stable, fairer environments, compared with less established owners, who worked their slaves harder and kept them in worse conditions.

Divisions existed even among the slaves themselves: field hands would work up to or in excess of 12 hours each day, allowed perhaps a half-day on a Saturday and a full day's rest on Sunday. House slaves, on the other hand, were regarded almost as one of the owner's family and enjoyed better living conditions as a result.

Force was at the heart of the system, however, the most common punishment being the whip, wielded by either a black driver or a white overseer. Whippings typically consisted of 20 or 30 lashes, with

50 or so for more serious misdemeanours. Punishment was carried out in public as an warning to the other slaves.

On rare occasions, resentment over the treatment of slaves would boil over into open revolt. In 1831, Nat Turner, a slave owned by a wealthy Virginian farmer, Joseph Travis, lead what became known as Nat Turner's Rebellion. Over the space of three months, never involving more than around 60 or so armed men, Turner was able to kill 55 whites, though in the end he was cornered and captured, and Turner and 17 of his followers were hanged. In a white backlash against the slaves, up to 200 lost their lives, but the 'rebellion' had terrified the white population and rumours spread of even larger uprisings across the South.

There had been other such attempts earlier in the 19th century, notably by Gabriel Prosser in 1800 and Denmark Vessy in 1822, but neither turned into actual revolts. These were rare, as had been the case at the height of the Roman Empire, but when the Union troops flooded into the Southern states during the American Civil War, such was the reaction from freed slaves that 180,000 or more donned the blue of the Union to fight against their former masters.

The South was not full of aristocrats as Hollywood would have us believe, and the vast majority of white farmers did not own slaves. They farmed at subsistence levels, unable to afford the investment in slaves needed to grow more lucrative crops. The basic foodstuffs were corn, sweet potatoes, peas and beans, supplemented by chickens and eggs, while game and fish could be had for free. Above all, they were fiercely independent and suspicious of outsiders.

While rice, tobacco, cotton and sugar were the main cash crops in the Deep South, wheat and other cereal crops were more common in the Northern states. New Orleans was central to the trade between North and South and there was a mutual dependency, which for some time had cemented the states together as a Union.

Gradually, over the years, the South began to set itself apart from the Northern states, and its importance as a producer of

further stagnation of the South's economy.

The simple fact was that subsistence farmers, though not exactly poor, did not produce enough to sell on the open market, which meant that the towns and cities were underdeveloped, being merely service centres for the cash crops of cotton and tobacco. Slavery added to the problem: slaves produced cash-generating crops, but the money went to their owners. The South could feed itself, but do little else.

In the North, meanwhile, in the two decades preceding the Civil War, rapid changes were afoot that would see an enormous gulf widen between North and South. In New York, New Jersey, Pennsylvania and New England, factories and mills were springing up, and manufacturing was developing even in the agricultural Midwest. But as for the South, the industrial revolution sweeping the United States had virtually passed it by. Apart from a few cotton mills and simple processing facilities for flour, tobacco and wood, the South was falling behind, and it would remain a predominantly agricultural economy.

By 1860 some 85 per cent of the South's workforce laboured in the fields, compared with only 40 per cent in the North and West. Only ten per cent of the population in the South lived in large towns or cities,

FAR LEFT: Eli Whitney was the inventor of a cotton gin in 1794, which speeded the removal of seeds from cotton and led to cotton's eventual mass-production.

BELOW: Slaves performing the laborious task of removing the seeds from newly-picked cotton.

cotton, with its attendant reliance on slavery, was to encourage this feeling of superiority. In 1800 the United States exported 40 per cent of its entire crop of 200,000 bales of cotton, with production reaching 2 million bales each year by the end of the 1830s. Two decades later and this had increased to 3 million bales and it had reached almost 5 million by the beginning of the American Civil War.

Farms in Tennessee, Kentucky, Maryland and North Carolina grew tobacco, and the low-lying regions of Georgia and South Carolina rice, but cotton was king. The cotton would be planted in the spring and early summer, and would be harvested in the fall and early winter, when towns and cities would be filled to bursting with bales of cotton, waiting to begin their long journey to eventual markets, either in the North or in Europe.

By this time, both North and South were losing population to the West, as day after day more virgin territory was being opened up and the Native Americans were being driven from their traditional lands. This drain would soon contribute to the

DIXIE, THE OLD SOUTH

RIGHT: A family of slaves.

OPPOSITE ABOVE: Woodcut depicting the revolt of Nat Turner, an American slave and leader of an 1831 rebellion of slaves in Southampton County, Virginia.

OPPOSITE BELOW: **The Abolition of the Slave Trade**
Cartoon of 1792 by Isaac Cruikshank, depicting the inhumanity of the slave trade. It shows Captain John Kimber, of Bristol, England, ill-treating a young black girl of 15.

compared with over 25 per cent elsewhere. Southern towns were tiny by Northern standards, being virtually dead except at harvest time, when they temporarily sprang to life. Moreover, the South, being predominantly agricultural, had to buy its manufactured goods either from the North or from Europe.

There were some Southerners who could see the danger of allowing the North not only to be the manufacturing base of the country, but also the principal point of entry for goods from abroad. But the wealth of the South lay in the hands of a few: these few large plantation owners had everything

to lose and nothing to gain from a change in the status quo.

These wealthy planters felt that industry, if it came to the South, would create a new wealthy class that would challenge their power. They continued to reinvest their surplus cash into more land and slaves, while the transport infrastructure, though adequate to deal with crops, could not compete with that of the North. Labour was also seen as a potential problem: to get subsistence farmers to work in industry they would have to be paid high wages, the alternative being slaves, who were expensive to buy and needed a higher initial

investment. They realized that industry would attract cheap immigrant labour and that if they allowed slaves to be hired out to the manufacturers they would lack the overall control they had previously enjoyed. As a representative of the planters, John Hammand remarked: 'Whenever a slave is made a mechanic he is more than half freed, and soon becomes, as we too well know, and all history attests, with rare exceptions, the most corrupt and turbulent of his class.'

The South may not have liked it, and may even have denied it, but it realized it was reliant on the North and on Europe. Nevertheless, the land provided the common farmer with sufficient food to feed his family and provided a handsome profit for the large land-owning, slave-holding class. Unlike most of the rest of the United States, the South chose to stay comparatively unchanging and unchanged.

It was clear to new immigrants to the United States that the South had little to offer in the way of opportunity, so they gravitated to the North and West. This was another loss to the South; as enormous opportunities for progress passed it by, so the rigid caste system bound it to the past.

The Southern white population, in what was in reality a backward and rural society, had learned how to be self-reliant, though it had not developed beyond the basic requirements of frontier life. The South was immersed in violence, the inherent violence of slavery, with a white population that feared its own downfall if it were ever to lose control over its slaves. In other words, the end of slavery would ultimately make it subordinate to an 'inferior race'. Abolitionists, therefore, represented the enemy, intent on exposing the South to murderous mobs of freed blacks. They had to be stopped, whatever the means, otherwise the survival of the South lay in the balance.

Violence was endemic. A gentleman would duel with an adversary, horsewhip an inferior and would fight, no holds barred, until one of them was reduced to a bloody pulp. Southerners had the reputation of being good officers and equally good soldiers, and individual military skills were highly regarded. In a sparsely populated rural environment it was not the done thing to have a formal education: in 1850 illiteracy stood at 20 per cent, compared with less than half a per cent in New England.

The wealthy provided private tutors for their children and further education for boys was at the military academies. Northern teachers and Northern literature were considered to be subversive.

Gradually, over the decades, Southern nationalism began to gain momentum in the slave-owning states. Some based their views on the argument that slavery freed white men from manual and boring duties, postulating that all whites in a slave state were aristocrats and needed to be served. They looked at the turmoil and chaos in the North and saw the South as a haven of peace and tranquillity. Above all, the 'aristocratic' Southerners, who held the bulk of the land and made their profits from slavery, saw their class as a noble elite. They were self-made men, and had a right to their position in society through their ownership of land and slaves.

Others even held the view that Northern industrialists were more immoral than the slave-owners of the South, in that they paid low wages while keeping most of the profits for themselves. The Southerner, on the other hand, obviously took less of the profits, in that he looked after his slaves and ensured they wanted for nothing.

Thus the South developed its own distinctive spin on life; it now sought independence in the belief that its society was superior to that of the North – unique, distinctive and worth fighting for. The North, it believed, was bent on destroying the South and all it stood for, therefore abolitionists, Northern politicians and even the Northern population at large were the sworn enemies of the South.

As events lurched towards the year 1861 and the outbreak of civil war, the South would be expected to prove more than its nationalistic aspirations; it would have to prove its military supremacy to gain the status it so earnestly desired.

CHAPTER TWO
THE CALL FOR ABOLITION

RIGHT: **Am I not a Man and a Brother?**
Woodcut.
An illustration for John Greenleaf Whittier's poem, 'Our Countrymen in Chains', of 1837. The design was originally the seal of the Society for the Abolition of Slavery in England in the 1780s, and appeared on medallions made for the society by Josiah Wedgwood.

BELOW RIGHT: William Lloyd Garrison, a radical abolitionist and editor of the newspaper, The Liberator*, was one of the founders of the American Anti-Slavery Society.*

On Saturday, 1 January 1831, the first issue of *The Liberator* was published in Boston, Massachusetts. This was a pro-abolitionist newspaper published by William Lloyd Garrison and Isaac Knapp. In the first issue, Garrison wrote: 'Urge we not to use moderation in a cause like the present. I am in earnest – I will not equivocate – I will not excuse – I will not retreat a single inch – AND I WILL BE HEARD. The apathy of the people is enough to make every statue leap from its pedestal, and to hasten the resurrection of the dead.'

Garrison was preaching to the converted. His tiny readership consisted of either African-Americans in the North or fellow white abolitionists. But he persisted,

hoping to bring his views to a wider audience. As the word spread, Southerners began to fear slave revolts and more people became convinced that slavery needed to be abolished. Garrison was not the first to believe that slavery had no place in a Christian society.

Back in 1746 a Quaker, John Woolman, visited the Southern states and saw his fellow Quakers using slaves. Deeply troubled by what he had seen, he convinced the Society of Friends to publish a statement in favour of emancipation and in 1754 published his own views on slavery in *Some Considerations on the Keeping of Negroes.* Quakers soon became some of the most vociferous critics of slavery and many more wrote pamphlets condemning the practice.

But Quakers were not the only religious group to consider slavery a sin. In 1780 the Methodists also came out against slavery, a handful of them having already freed their slaves; five years later, Methodists still holding slaves would be excommunicated.

By the end of the 18th century, Congregationalists, Baptists and Presbyterians had joined the Quakers and Methodists in their condemnation of slavery. All made statements against slavery, and urged their members to free their slaves and take up active roles in anti-slavery societies. There were also early attempts to phase out slavery gradually rather than immediately. The Presbyterian clergyman, David Rice, from Kentucky, proposed that states should import no more slaves, free those born after 1792 and then gradually free the rest. His published view, *Slavery Inconsistent with Justice and Good Policy,* also played on the notion that an enslaved body of people was always a threat to the Republic, and could be expected to rise up one day and overthrow the state.

The great paradox of slavery lay at the very heart of the American Revolution and the Declaration of Independence. When Thomas Jefferson wrote the first draft, his intention was to condemn slavery. He blamed the English, and principally George III, who had vetoed laws passed by the state of Virginia against the importation of slaves.

The declaration enshrined the noble ideals of universal equality and basic human rights. But there was a huge inconsistency in the way these ideals were put into practice, in that while the British were held to be denying Americans the right to direct their own affairs, the Americans themselves were guilty of enslavement of another kind. Once

In 1864 George N. Barnard was made the official photographer for the United States Army, Chief Engineer's Office, Division of the Mississippi. He followed Union General William T. Sherman's infamous March to the Sea and in 1866 published an album of 61 photographs, 'Photographic Views of Sherman's Campaign'. This is a photograph taken in Whitehall Street, Atlanta, Georgia, shortly after Sherman had taken the city in 1864.

THE CALL FOR ABOLITION

RIGHT: *'Get off the Track', a song for emancipation, composed by Jesse Hutchinson, Jr. The song was dedicated to the anti-slavery editor Nathanial Peabody Rogers.*

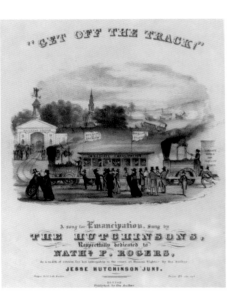

RIGHT: **Pioneers of Freedom**
features individual portraits of Charles Sumner, Henry Ward Beecher, Wendell Phillips, William Lloyd Garrison, Gerrit Smith, Horace Greeley and Henry Wilson. Circa 1866.

CENTRE: **The Sale**
A card painted by Henry Louis Stephens of an African-American slave being sold. Circa 1863.

FAR RIGHT: **The Parting – Buy us Too!**
Card by the same artist, showing an African-American slave being separated from his family. Circa 1863.

recognized as such, the inconsistency could only find a remedy in the spread and implementation of anti-slavery beliefs.

This, however, was a slow process. The Continental Congress, during the revolutionary war itself, banned the importation of slaves in 1774, and in the North, where slavery had never been as widespread, abolition slowly took effect over the next three decades. Vermont and New Hampshire led the way and Rhode Island and Connecticut followed in 1784. Pennsylvania abolished slavery in 1780 but found constant policing was required to stamp it out, while Massachusetts, with a slave population of three per cent, made the practice illegal in 1790. It took until 1799 to pass the necessary legislation in New York, however, and New Jersey followed suit in 1804. Both of these states had a slave population of between eight and 12 per cent.

But this did not make all slaves free: there was the question of reimbursing the slave-owners. To avoid this, slaves got their freedom after a period of time had elapsed, and some had to wait for nearly 30 years.

Despite the progress made in the North, slave-owners themselves held the balance of power in the South, and simply ignored the abolitionists. Thomas Jefferson led the movement to prevent slavery from establishing itself in the Western territories when the North-West Ordnance was passed in 1787, and he was instrumental in ensuring the foreign trade in slaves was brought to an end, it being officially outlawed on 1 January 1808.

Having 'defeated' slavery in the North, the abolitionist movement began to lose its way in the 1820s, being content to approach the issue by tackling it in small, measured steps. Churches still existed that advocated excommunication for slave-owners, but others repealed or simply ignored the requirement not to hold slaves. Although it was generally believed that the moral cause had been won, it was also believed that slave-owners would come around to a similar way of thinking given time.

An odd mix of abolitionists, politicians and slave-owners set up the American Colonization Society in 1816. They proposed to give slaves the opportunity to set up a Christian state in West Africa. Called Liberia, the new republic would prove that a slave, once freed, could be as civilized as any white person. But it is clear that others saw this as a means of ridding the United States of its ex-slaves once and for all.

Congress passed the first Fugitive Slave Act in 1793. This made it dangerous to help runaway slaves, though many continued to do so all the same. An even more draconian act was passed in 1850, making those aiding

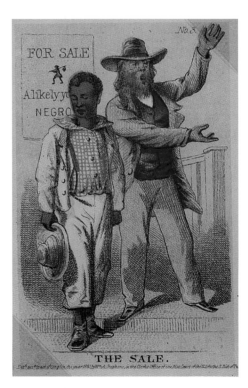

and abetting the escape of a slave subject to a $1,000 fine. Runaway slaves escaping from the South rarely lingered in the Northern states, especially if they lacked the necessary documents proving they were free. The first safe destination, being slave-free, was therefore Canada, whence a sea passage could be taken to the West Indies.

During this period, an active minority was directly involved in helping as many abolitionists, Quakers, and freed and fugitive slaves fleeing bounty hunters, as possible, the Rev. John Rankin, of Ripley, Ohio, being one of these. His organization, known as the Underground Railroad, provided a network of guides and safe houses stretching from the South to the Northern states and beyond.

It is not known how many were saved by the actions of the Underground Railroad, though estimates range between 25 and 100,000. Whatever the figure, it was a drop in the ocean, and most slaves would have had to wait for the Union army to free them or until the Civil War had been won.

Although Rankin is credited with setting up a loose network of escape roots, others made even greater efforts. Foremost among these was Harriet Tubman, herself an escaped slave from Maryland, who became the 'Moses' of her people and guided thousands to safety both before and during the Civil War. Others include Livi Coffin and Isaac Hopper, while Thomas Garrett is credited with assisting 3,000 fugitive slaves.

Slaves had been attending Evangelical Christian Churches, led by white missionaries and supported by benevolent societies, since the 1790s. Gradually, however, their own African Methodist Episcopal Church was established. Its first bishop was Richard Allen, who led attacks on the American Colonization Society and helped to found a Negro Convention Movement.

By the time Garrison published his *Liberator* in 1831, the majority of his readership was black. Printing presses spread political thought to the far-flung corners of the United States, and abolitionists would use this revolution in

communications to give fresh life to their cause. Garrison found a willing partner in Benjamin Lundy – a Quaker who had sold his saddle-making business to found his own anti-slavery newspaper, *The Genius of Universal Emancipation*, first published in 1821. Lundy managed to limp along financially, at the same time publicizing the Convention for Promoting the Abolition of Slavery among other abolitionist groups.

The two had collaborated with one another for a short time after they met in 1828. But Lundy supported colonizing Mexico with freed slaves, while Garrison was against colonization and wished to see an outright end to slavery. Garrison published his arguments in 1832 in *Thoughts on African Colonization*, in which he roundly attacked all factions of the American Colonization Society and called for immediate emancipation. He strongly believed that slave-owners would never relinquish their slaves until they accepted it as sinful to hold another man in bondage.

In many ways Garrison echoed the views of British abolitionists, who had effected the end of slavery in the West Indies, where they had won the moral argument. In his discussions with Northern blacks it had become clear to Garrison that almost all of them were against colonization. It was also obvious that they despised slave-owners and believed them undeserving of a voice in the debate.

Meanwhile, Arthur and Lewis Tappan, wealthy New York merchants implacably opposed to slavery, called a meeting in 1831. The outcome was the creation of the New England Anti-Slavery Society, and its members were heavily influenced by Garrison's anti-colonization views and even more so by the British government, when it abolished slavery in 1833.

The New England group now sought to spread its views across the nation. On 4 December 1833, 63 people met in Philadelphia to establish the American Anti-Slavery Society. Significantly, three of the delegates were black men and four were white women.

They were all Evangelical Christians,

Protestants with strong moral principles. Their focus was the Declaration of Independence, which says that 'all men are created equal'. In the South this was still clearly not the case, and they advocated immediate emancipation without compensation. This was a radical departure,

Photograph of Harriet Tubman, also known as Grandma Moses, the African-American freedom fighter.

RIGHT: John Quincy Adams (1767–1848), President of the United States from 1825–45, and himself the son of a president. He is most famous for his formulation of the Monroe Doctrine.

FAR RIGHT: James Birney became secretary of the American Anti-Slavery Society in 1837.

BELOW RIGHT: **Abolition of the Slave Trade or The Man, the Master** *A British print showing the roles of slave and master reversed, 1789.*

rather than a mainstream view, and could easily have floundered at its inception. Four years later, however, New York had 274 such societies, Massachusetts 145 and Ohio 213. By 1838 there were 250,000 members in 1,350 societies. To spread the word and arrange the establishment of new societies, the group had over 60 agents on the road, all of whom espoused immediate emancipation.

Pamphlets and journals supported the work of the agents. The national society, in 1838, produced a staggering 647,000 copies of various papers, tracts and pamphlets, while *The Liberator* had been joined by up to 40 other newspapers.

The movement used a petition system to encourage members. The names of those who signed the petition were published; politicians could see the names of voters on the lists and those who had not yet signed saw that the House of Representatives was being bombarded with abolitionist demands.

During the period 1837 to 1838, Congress received petitions bearing 414,000 signatures. The language of the petitions was designed to be provocative: slavery was described as a crime, one that corrupted the

ABOLITION OF THE SLAVE TRADE, OR THE MAN THE MASTER.

of Garrison, as a fugitive from justice, while Louisiana placed a price of $50,000 on Arthur Tappan. Southern politicians begged their Northern counterparts to do something to stop publication and distribution of what they saw as incendiary material, their fear being that the writings and actions of the abolitionists would encourage a slave rebellion. The South effectively tried to ban written or spoken abolitionist beliefs, imprisoning some, firing others and whipping a few when they were caught.

There had been an attempt to ignore the abolitionist petitions in 1834. The senate had been having long and involved discussions on the subject of slavery, while former President John Quincy Adams of Massachusetts led attacks against the 'gag rule', which ignored the petitions, seeing them as a threat to American liberty. The Southerners were forced to defend every criticism of slavery, which ultimately led to a tailing-off of Northern sympathy. The gag rule was finally lifted in 1845.

There were as many as 165 anti-abolitionist riots in the period 1833 to 1838, some violent, others in the form of heckling

FAR LEFT: **Distinguished Colored Men**
First published c.1883 by A. Muller & Co. It features Frederick Douglass, Robert Brown Elliott, Blanche K. Bruce, William Wells Brown, Prof. R.T. Greener, Rt. Rev. Richard Allen, J.H. Rainey, E.D. Basset, John Mercer Langston, P.B.S. Pinchback and Henry Highland Garnet.

BELOW LEFT: **The Fugitive's Song**
Lithograph, 1845.
Sheet music illustrated with a portrait of the prominent black abolitionist, Frederick Douglass, in the guise of a runaway slave.

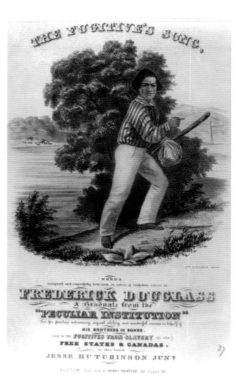

American way of life and which it was cowardice to ignore.

The abolitionists tried to force religious bodies and reform societies to adopt an anti-slavery stance, and every success further promoted their cause. Each time one refused, however, they were bombarded with accusations of hypocrisy or cowardice, which caused enormous rifts within the churches. The Presbyterian Church split in 1837, the Methodist Episcopal Church in both 1842 and 1844 and the Baptists in

1845. In most cases the split followed a North-South divide.

But the abolitionists did not have it all their own way. In 1832 the Connecticut state legislature blocked the establishment of a mixed-race girls' school in Canterbury, leading to the arrest of the Quaker teacher, Prudence Crandel.

Meanwhile, the South refused to take this lying down; it was affronted by the attacks of the abolitionists. Georgia, for example, put a price of $5,000 on the head

to Alton, Illinois, where his presses had been wrecked on three occasions. When the mob attacked a fourth time, his warehouse was burned down, his press was thrown into the Ohio river and Lovejoy was shot five times.

The South had been forced to make compromises in the past, but now there was nothing that could satisfy its opponents.

ABOVE: Frederick Douglass.

ABOVE RIGHT: The killing of Elijah Lovejoy, journalist and abolitionist, at Alton, Illinois, in 1837.

RIGHT: The resurrection of Henry Box Brown, who escaped from Richmond, Virginia, in a box. Here, he emerges from the box in the office of Pennsylvania's Anti-Slavery Society. Present is Frederick Douglass (left) holding a claw hammer.

or throwing rotten eggs. Abolitionists' homes were attacked, presses were destroyed and individuals beaten up.

James Birney was forced out of Kentucky in the 1830s and made for Cincinnati, desperate to see his anti-slavery newspaper, the *Philanthropist*, published. Despite warnings from abolitionists he went ahead and on 30 July 1836 the printing presses were destroyed by a mob. Garrison was attacked in Boston in October 1835 and Elijah Lovejoy was murdered in Illinois in 1837. Lovejoy had fled Missouri and moved

THE RESURRECTION OF HENRY BOX BROWN AT PHILADELPHIA.
Who escaped from Richmond Va. in a Box. 3 feet long 2½ ft deep and 2 ft wide

THE CIVIL WAR

This was because the call for abolition had not come from the established politicians, with whom the South could have debated and brought about a mutually acceptable outcome. The abolitionists were outside this world; they were aspiring politicians, community leaders and worse, educated blacks, with whom the South had no hope of ever reaching a compromise.

Direct, aggressive action to silence abolitionists did not work either. In murdering Lovejoy, the abolitionists had been handed a martyr on a plate. In fact, the South formed four abolitionist groups. First there were the radicals, typified by Garrison and Wendell Phillips, who were not only opposed to slavery, but to various institutions and values that allowed it to exist. The second group were the Ecclesiasticals, such as the Methodist, Orange Scott, who constantly criticized slavery and promoted a strong distaste for pro-slavery principles. The third group were the political abolitionists, Birney being a leading example, who was nominated for president at the Liberty Party convention in New York in 1840. The party believed that existing parties were too wedded to the slave-owners to ever press for abolition. Birney lost heavily in the 1840 presidential election and faired little better four years later.

The final group were the black abolitionists, some of whom also belonged to the other three groups. A network of black organizations had sprung up and their key role was to shame their white colleagues into pushing harder, using the black abolitionists' personal experiences of slavery and racial prejudice. Frederick Douglass was perhaps the best-known former slave, who had established strong political connections and lectured widely. He published an influential newspaper (first called the *North Star* and later *Frederick Douglass's Paper*) between 1847 and 1860.

The issue of slavery had been moving in and out of national politics ever since the American Revolution, gradually becoming a dominant issue, but deadlock and crisis were hanging in the air as the United States entered the 1850s. Northern radicals, like Abraham Lincoln of Illinois and Joshua Giddings, were pressing for abolition in the District of Columbia, while, as yet, nothing had been decided about the new territories of California and New Mexico, which had gone to the U.S. following the Mexican War.

Meanwhile, the comparative power of North and South was still shifting in favour of the North and policy against the interests of the South was still being made.

CHAPTER THREE

THE BREAKAWAY BEGINS

RIGHT: James Buchanan (1791–1868) was the 15th president of the United States, from 1856–61.

BELOW RIGHT: The abolitionist John Brown led an armed crusade against slavery, which ended in his execution at Harper's Ferry in 1859, and was an important event in the beginnings of the American Civil War

The year 1850 saw a large number of major issues still waiting to be resolved and for a time the dissolution of the Union seemed to be the only way forward. The exact nature of the territories taken from the Mexicans needed careful thought, the debt and size of Texas required consideration, and there was the problem of slaves being sold in sight of the capitol in the District of Columbia and the increasing numbers of fugitive slaves. The result was the Missouri Compromise of 1850.

California would be admitted into the Union as a free state and the question of slavery in Utah and New Mexico would be left to the electorate. The Federal government would shoulder the debts of the former independent Texas and slavery would

continue in the District of Columbia, but there would be an end to the slave trade. The main objection was the newly proposed Fugitive Slave Act. Northerners refused to exact the requirements of the law: heavy fines for those who helped slaves and the denial of the fugitive's right to a trial. The South, however, was unwilling to accept any of the compromises unless the North complied. Southern elections in 1850 and 1851 heavily supported pro-compromise candidates, consequently the compromises set out by Henry Cley of Kentucky were more or less agreed.

There are several examples of Northerners defying the Fugitive Slave Act, as in the case of the slave, Shadrach (Boston, 1 February 1851). In each case, mobs of abolitionists worked to ensure that slaves remained free and were spirited out of the country.

By 1854 it seemed as though the pro-slavery lobby was winning the war of words and deeds, when the states of Nebraska and Kansas came up for debate. The result, after much political wrangling, was that the two states should be allowed to choose whether they adopted slavery or not. More seriously, Southerners were behind the proposed purchase or seizure of Cuba from the Spanish; this, too, was to be a slave state, but in the end nothing came of the plan.

Settlers from the Eastern states were flowing into Kansas, as were even more from the South, and it was to become the fighting ground of the pro-slavery factions against the abolitionists. The 'free-state' settlers received harassment from the South, intent on making Kansas a slave state. Militant free-staters, like John Brown, called for men and weapons to protect the state of Kansas, where a civil war was all too likely; in the spring of 1856 a pro-slavery mob attacked the free-state town of Lawrence and sacked it. John Brown, in response, attacked the pro-slavery settlers in Pottawotomie, and the pro-slavers then plundered southern Kansas, where Brown lived. The fighting continued well into the summer of 1856.

President Buchanan came to power in 1856, promising to settle the slave question once and for all, and hoping to obtain a speedy resolution to the Kansas civil war. Just two days after Buchanan's inaugural speech, the Supreme Court passed a judgement on the Dred Scott case, the results of which were to have long-lasting and dangerous implications. Dred Scott was the slave of a doctor who had joined the army in 1834. Posted to Illinois and then to Wisconsin, Scott had lived for 24 years in states where there was no slavery.

Consequently, Scott's case hinged on these facts when he sued for freedom after his owner died. The Lower Missouri court found in Scott's favour, but the State Supreme Court found against him. He contested the case in the Federal District Court and then the Supreme Court. The Supreme Court ruled that a slave was not a citizen. Scott had been a slave in a slave state when the action had been brought, making the four years out of Missouri irrelevant. In short, Congress could not deprive a citizen of his property without due process of law. In effect, the court declared the Missouri Compromise unconstitutional.

Abraham Lincoln was nominated as the Republican candidate for president on 16 June 1858, making his famous 'House Divided' speech soon after. In it he stated that the divisions in the United States threatened to tear the Union apart, and that it simply could not survive being 'half-slave and half-free'. He accepted that slavery was spreading and pledged to reverse the trend.

In the middle of the electioneering, news came that John Brown and his followers had mounted an attack on the Federal arsenal at Harper's Ferry, Virginia, on 16 October 1859. Brown's plan was incredible: with just 13 white men and five black supporters he intended to seize the weapons in the arsenal and set up a fortified base, with himself as

ROBERT EDWARD LEE (1807–70)

Lee was born in Stratford, Virginia, the son of General Henry Lee. His father died when he was 11 but Lee was determined to follow in his father's footsteps as a soldier. He entered West Point in 1825 and graduated in 1829. By 1834 he had been made a chief engineer and became a first lieutenant two years later, a captain in 1838, and by 1844 was one of the board of visitors at West Point. He was assigned to General Scott's personal staff during the Mexican War and is credited with positioning the American batteries at Vera Cruz and other engagements. Lee was in Washington in October 1859 and was given the responsibility of dealing with John Brown's raiding party at Harper's Ferry. In March 1861 Lee was offered the command of the Union army but he could not, in his heart, draw his sword against his own state, and resigned his commission in April. Initially he was assigned to Georgia,

South Carolina and Florida. After the Battle of Seven Pines, when General Joseph Johnston was severely wounded, Lee was offered the command of the Army of Northern Virginia and threw himself straight into the new role, fighting the Seven Days' Battles, which effectively stopped McClellan from threatening Richmond. Lee became a hero of the South and was nicknamed 'Uncle Robert'. He beat the Union army at the Second Bull Run but the volume of casualties and attrition led to a stalemate at Antietam in September 1862. Lee was again successful at Fredericksburg in December and Chancellorsville in April 1863, but made costly mistakes at Gettysburg and again at Malvern Hill, and from mid-1864 was forced to fight a defensive campaign against the overwhelming strength of the Union army under Grant. Lee became Commander-in-Chief in January 1864 and successfully defended Richmond and Petersburg until April 1865, when, cornered and outnumbered, he surrendered his army at Appomattox Courthouse. After the war Lee applied for the post-war amnesty offered to former Confederates who swore to renew their allegiance to the United States. This was never granted, however, because his application was mislaid and was not uncovered until the 1970s. Lee died of heart disease in Lexington in October 1870, something he had been suffering from since 1863.

leader of a new provisional government. With this established, he would force emancipation. Colonel Robert E. Lee swiftly and effectively dealt with the raid. The two-day siege claimed the lives of two of Brown's sons and eight others and government losses were seven killed. Brown was arrested, tried and hanged on 2 December 1859. He would be immortalized in song, but as the *Richmond Inquirer* prophetically noted: 'The Harper's Ferry invasion has advanced the cause of disunion more than any other event that has happened since the formation of the government.'

The election campaign pressed on, with four candidates vying for the presidential votes. John Bell of Tennessee stood as the Constitutional Unionist candidate, John C. Breckinridge for the breakaway Southern Democrats, while Lincoln faced the Democrat, Stephen A. Douglas.

By early fall it was clear that the Republicans were winning the hearts of the voters. Election night was 6 November 1860 and Lincoln stormed ahead in an unassailable lead, snatching all the key Northern states. He received 180 electoral votes, a majority of 37. Douglas won just 12, Breckinridge 72 (all the slave states) and Bell 39.

Lincoln had received only 39.9 per cent of the popular vote, while together the Democrats had achieved 47 per cent and Bell 14. Had Breckinridge and Douglas run together, however, Lincoln would still have won 169 electoral votes, giving him a majority of 35.

The South had mixed feelings where Lincoln's victory was concerned, even though he came from a slave state and had strong links with the South. The strongest reaction came from South Carolina, which supported the right of the states to secede. In November it decided to call its election delegates to a meeting, and special convention elections would also take place in Alabama, Mississippi, Florida, Georgia and Louisiana. It was clear that secession was in the air, yet Lincoln had not even been inaugurated; Buchanan still held that post of president until it was handed over in March 1861.

On 3 December 1860 Buchanan, in his last annual message to Congress, had tried to diffuse the situation. He called on the people to see that the Southerners should be 'let alone and permitted to manage their domestic institutions in their own way'. He said this in the hope of allying the fears of the South, but added that he saw secession as illegal, in that 'such a principle is wholly inconsistent with the history as well as the character of the Federal Constitution'. Sitting firmly on the fence, he went on to say that the government did not have the right to prevent a state from leaving the Union: 'The power to make war against a state is at variance with the whole spirit and intentions of the Constitution. The fact is our Union rests upon public opinion, and can never be cemented by the blood of its citizens shed in a civil war.' Blood would be shed, oceans of

it. Buchanan's speech brought solace neither to the South nor the North; in fact it was a matter of concern to them both.

The House of Representatives rapidly created a Committee of Thirty-Three, one person representing each state, while Vice President Breckinridge created the Council of Thirteen in the Senate. The key objective of both committees was to douse the flames of secession and find yet another compromise that both sides could accept as palatable. On the very day that the Council of Thirteen was appointed (20 December), the South Carolina convention adopted an Ordnance of Secession, passed with a vote of 169 to nought. South Carolina published *A Declaration of the Immediate Causes of Secession*, along with an *Address to the Slaveholding States* (written by R. Barnwell Rhett). This action brought three Federal fortifications in the Charleston area into the national spotlight, the first being Fort Pinckney (close to Charleston), the second

OPPOSITE RIGHT: Stephen A. Douglas was responsible for the highly controversial Kansas-Nebraska Act of 1854 that revived the issue of slavery.

ABOVE LEFT: John C. Breckinridge (1821–85), the 14th Vice President of the United States from 1857–61, under Buchanan, and a Confederate general.

ABOVE: The interior of Fort Sumter, with James Island in the distance.

FAR LEFT: John Bell, Secretary of War from 1841.

LEFT: Fort Moultrie, Charleston, South Carolina.

THE BREAKAWAY BEGINS

A civilian-chartered paddle steamer, with Union troops on board, the *Star of the West*, came under heavy fire from South Carolina artillery as it attempted to reach the fort. After it had been hit twice, the paddle steamer turned back.

A week later, on 16 January 1861, the Georgia secession convention got underway, passing the Ordnance of Seccession by 208 votes to 89. Four days later the Louisiana convention met at Baton Rouge, and despite attempts to delay the decision, secession was agreed by 113 to 17.

The last state of the Deep South to secede was Texas. Governor Sam Houston was all for the state remaining in the Union and did his best to avert the assembly of a convention. It took place, nevertheless, in Austin on 28 January 1861, the inevitable result being 166 votes to eight in favour of secession.

On 4 February 1861, a Peace Convention assembled in Washington with hopes of reversing the secession decisions and reaching a compromise to save the Union. On the same day, delegates from the

Fort Moultrie (on Sullivan's Island) and the unfinished Fort Sumter.

The Federal government, wary of the possibilities of secession, had begged for reinforcements to be sent to the area. Now South Carolina was demanding the surrender of the forts. Major Robert Anderson, who was in command of the forts, moved his forces to the one that was more defendable, Sumter, on the basis that it was the hardest to attack.

On 9 January 1861 Mississippi voted to secede, with a vote of 84 to 15, and Florida followed suit the following day, voting 62 to 7 in favour of secession. Alabama was next on 11 January, with a pro-secession vote of 61 to 39.

Meanwhile, the Council of Thirteen was still hard at work, desperately seeking to avert disaster. John J. Crittenden proposed a compromise plan to save the Union, but in the end the committee rejected his proposal by seven votes to six. By 28 December the committee was clear that no reconciliation plan could be agreed. Crittenden made more proposals to the senate in early January, three of which the Council of Thirteen accepted: the proper enforcement of the Fugitive Slave Law; an amendment to the U.S. Constitution, stating there would be no interference with slavery where it already existed; and the right of fugitive slaves to a trial by jury.

Several of President Buchanan's cabinet members resigned in late December as their states seceded from the Union. Unionists from the North replaced them, the most significant being the new Attorney General, Edwin M. Stanton. Stanton took a firm line against the secessionists from the start and would be invaluable to Lincoln in later years.

Attempts were made to reinforce the beleaguered Major Anderson and his men at Fort Sumter, but it was a poorly kept secret.

THE CIVIL WAR

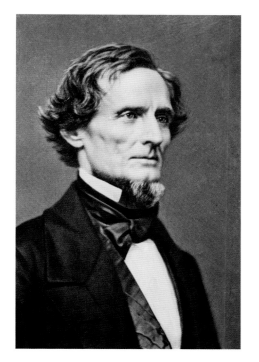

seceded states met in Montgomery, Alabama, to create the Confederate States of America. By 8 February they had drafted a new constitution and selected Jefferson Davis of Mississippi as the first provisional president of the Confederacy. Alexander H. Stephens became the vice president, taking the oath of office three days later. Shortly afterwards, Davis formally became president and he made his inaugural address, in which he stated: 'We have changed the constituent parts, but not the system of our government. The Constitution formed by our fathers is that of these Confederate states.'

The Peace Convention finally made seven compromise proposals on 27 February, but it was too little too late and what remained was to see how Abraham Lincoln would react, once he became president of what remained of the United States.

On paper, if there was to be war, the vast imbalance between North and South should have made the result a foregone conclusion. The 23 states loyal to the Union (including Kansas) had a population of 22 million, while in the 11 Confederate states, the white population numbered 5.5 million, with a further 3.5 million slaves. Only 9,000 of the 30,000 miles (48300km) of railroad track lay

within the South, while 75 per cent of the nation's factories were in the North, together with the vast majority of shipyards and overwhelming proportions of coal and iron.

Virginia finally voted for secession on 17 April, closely followed by Arkansas, North Carolina and Tennessee. Importantly, however, Delaware, Maryland, Kentucky and Missouri, all slave states, remained loyal to the Union, though many inhabitants of these four border states did travel south and joined the Confederate forces.

The population and materials imbalance was in part offset by the quality of the Southern rank and file and of its officers. Southern men could ride and shoot, and Southern gentlemen were accustomed to commanding men.

Around 30 per cent of the regular Union army officer corps joined the Confederacy, including two men who would become icons of the Confederate armies, Robert E. Lee and Thomas 'Stonewall' Jackson. The regular army, rank and file, remained largely loyal, but was a drop in the ocean and only numbered some 16,000 men.

FAR LEFT: The Confederate President Jefferson Davis.

LEFT: The Confederate General Joseph E. Johnston.

BELOW LEFT: **Portrait of Thomas Jonathan Jackson on Horseback** *Reproduction of a painting of Thomas Stonewall Jackson, c.1913.*

ABOVE: The Federal Major General Robert Patterson.

ABOVE RIGHT: The Confederate General Pierre G.T. Beauregard.

RIGHT: The Federal General George Brinton McClellan.

clearly referred to Fort Sumter, still holding out in Charleston harbour. Lincoln ordered supplies to be taken to the fort, but before they arrived by ship, the Confederate guns had opened up on the fort. It was 12 April and the next day, with no ammunition left, Fort Sumter surrendered.

On 15 April Lincoln issued the order to muster 75,000 militia with a length of service of 90 days. On 3 May he called up 40,034 men to provide the regular army with 22,714 more men and the rest were allocated to the navy.

Meanwhile, on 16 April, the Confederate government passed a motion to introduce the conscription of all white men between the ages of 18 and 35 years.

It soon became clear to Lincoln that he would need considerable numbers of men and a great deal of money to bring a swift end to the war. He asked for 400,000 men and $400m. These vast numbers were for the future; what was more pressing was that Washington was just over the Potomac river from Confederate Virginia, and to defend it he would need to rely on only 30,000 or so men, commanded by General Irvin McDowell.

It was an army in name only, in that it was a ragbag of volunteer regiments, mainly former militiamen. Very few of

In April 1861 a North Carolina newspaper identified the key differences between the armies of the North and South: 'The army of the South will be composed of the best material that ever made up an army; whilst that of Lincoln will be gathered from the sewers of the cities – the degraded, beastly off-scourings of all quarters of the world, who will serve for pay, and run away when danger threatens them.' This was very close to the mark, as the North would soon discover.

Lincoln was finally inaugurated president on 4 March 1861 and, unlike the hesitant Buchanan, resolved to deal with the secession crisis. Lincoln insisted he had no desire to interfere with slavery but that he would execute the law in all the states. He considered the Union to be unbroken. He would order the holding, occupying and possession of government property. This

them had ever fired at anything other than a target and were complete novices where drill or battlefield manoeuvres were concerned.

The opposing armies faced off with Confederate General Pierre G.T. Beauregard at Manassas Junction, with 20,000 men. General George B. McClellan had a Union army of 20,000 in Virginia and a further 13,000 based at Harper's Ferry under General Patterson. Facing Patterson was General Joseph E. Johnston's force of 10,000 Confederates.

Lincoln ordered McDowell's 30,000 to advance, while Patterson would check Johnston. Lincoln figured that McDowell's army would be more than sufficient to deal with Beauregard's 20,000 men.

It seemed like peacetime manoeuvres as McDowell's men began to close on Manassas Junction on 20 July 1861. The next day McDowell ordered his leading units to cross a small stream known as Bull Run.

THE CIVIL WAR

Raided by John Brown in 1859, this is Harper's Ferry, West Virginia, as it appears today.

CHAPTER FOUR
BULL RUN TO GETTYSBURG

The First Battle of Bull Run, a sketch showing the position of Captain F.B. Schaeffer's command along the Bull Run, 600 yards from the Lewis house on 21 July 1861.

The Battle of Bull Run (or the First Battle of Manassas) began at 0515 on Sunday 21 July 1861, when a Union artillery piece sent a shell towards the Confederate lines. Most of the key future military leaders of the North and South were present at the battle, some in very junior positions.

The Union army, under McDowell, committed some 18,572 men and 24 guns to the fight. The Confederates, in two forces, the first under Beauregard and the second under Joseph E. Johnston, committed 9,713 and 8,340 men respectively.

The Union force advanced, hoping to catch the Confederates unawares, but met determined opposition instead. The Confederates gave ground until they met the Virginians under Jackson. It was at Bull Run that Thomas Jackson earned his nickname 'Stonewall'. He adamantly refused to budge and the rest of the wavering Confederate army rallied to his left and right.

It was at this point that McDowell made the error that cost him the battle. He ordered up artillery to bombard the stubborn Confederates, but faced strong batteries of Confederate artillery and got the worst of the exchange. Suddenly, the Confederate 33rd Virginia, dressed in blue, were mistaken for Union reserves and cut down the Union artillery crews. The 33rd then charged and routed several Union regiments, while Colonel J.E.B. Stuart's cavalry seized the abandoned Union artillery. Eventually the guns were recovered and McDowell began to feed in more troops, as did the Confederates. In the confused fight, Union troops were slipping away, back across Bull Run. Soon it turned into a rout. The Confederates had the field, seizing 5,000 muskets, half a million cartridges, 28 artillery pieces, countless

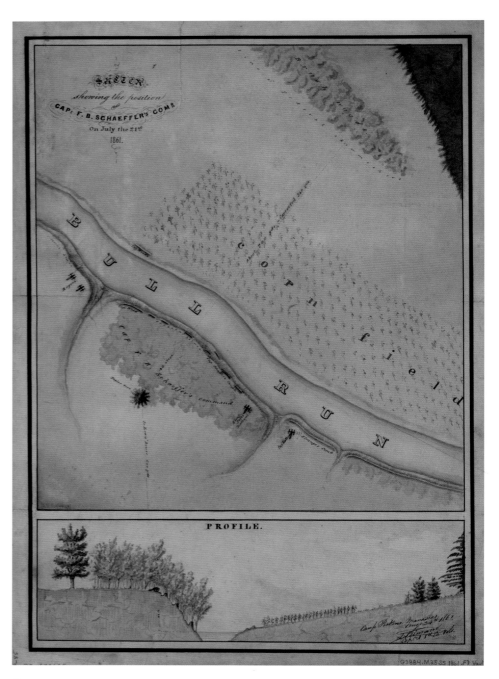

horses and masses of clothing and equipment.

The disaster cost McDowell his job and Major General George McClellan almost immediately replaced him. It was first blood to the Confederacy, the Union blockade of the South having been declared but not enforced. Early attacks on the Southern coastline were working, however, the seizure of the entrance to Port Royal, South Carolina, being particularly effective in November 1861.

For both sides it appeared that the control of the Mississippi river, as far as the Gulf, was essential. The first major battle took place on 10 August at Wilson's Creek, 10 miles (16km) from Springfield. Outnumbered, the Union forces were decisively defeated. The Union army rapidly reorganized and a new offensive was mounted in February 1862. By then, the Confederates had been reinforced and had 5,000 Native Americans in support. The two armies clashed at Pea Ridge, Arkansas, between 7 and 8 March, but the battle was complicated by the fact that the Native Americans scalped friend and foe alike. Despite this the Confederates were soundly beaten.

The Western Theatre brought two men

together who would eventually shape the war and bring military victory to the Union: Ulysses Simpson Grant and William Tecumseh Sherman.

Grant, an undistinguished West Point graduate, failed farmer, failed realtor and failed engineer, had received his appointment as a brigadier general on 7 August 1861. Sherman, who had fought at the First Bull Run as a colonel, would join him to seize control of the Tennessee river – a vital waterway running through northern Alabama, Tennessee, and Kentucky and into Ohio. The river provided a superb opportunity to drive into the Deep South.

Firstly, the defending forts, Henry and Donelson, needed to be taken, and Grant managed to achieve this in February 1862. Grant's overwhelming victory against the Confederates brought great hope to the North. The surrender negotiations with the Confederate commander, Buckner, also gave Grant his nickname (he would earn his second later – Butcher Grant): 'Yours of this date proposing armistice and appointment of commissioner to settle terms of capitulation is received. No terms except unconditional and immediate surrender can be accepted. I propose to move immediately on your works.'

Instantly, Ulysses S. Grant became Unconditional Surrender Grant, which would set the tone of his war. Grant took nearly 15,000 prisoners and he could now

ABOVE: View of the Bull Run river.

BELOW FAR LEFT: The Battle of Pea Ridge, Arkansas, 7 March 1862.

LEFT: Sheet music for the Pea Ridge March, dedicated to Major General Franz Sigel, composed by Chr. Bach. Lithograph by Kurz and Co., Milwaukee, Wisconsin.

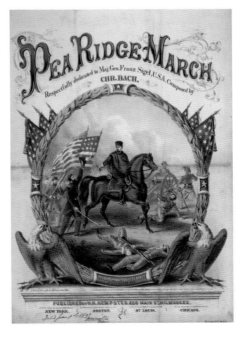

THE CIVIL WAR

The First Battle of Bull Run, 21 July 1861
The American School.
Lithograph published in 1889.
Collection of the New York Historical Society.

Battle of Pea Ridge, Arkansas, 7–8 March 1862

American School (19th Century).
Lithograph by Kurz & Allison.
Private collection.

The Battle of Shiloh, 1862
(Also known as the Battle of Pittsburg
Landing, 7–8 April 1862)
Lithograph by Kurz and Allison
(fl.1880–98).
Collection of the New York Historical
Society.

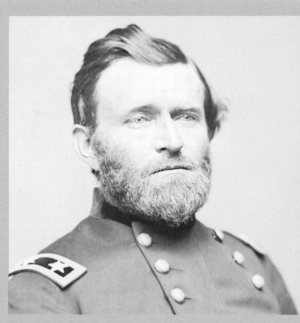

**HIRAM ULYSSES SIMPSON GRANT
(1822–85)**

Grant was born at Point Pleasant, Ohio. He was not considered to be particularly bright academically, but he entered West Point in 1839. This is where he discovered his name had been registered incorrectly and at that point dropped Hiram as a Christian name. He graduated twenty-first out of thirty-nine in 1843 and served with distinction during the Mexican War, where he was associated with Zachary Taylor and Winfield Scott. Grant resigned his commission in 1854 and worked as a clerk in his father's business, where there were rumours of heavy drinking and poor discipline. In May 1861 he was given command of a regiment of infantry, but by August he was a brigadier general. He earned his nickname, 'Unconditional Surrender' Grant, in February 1862, when he demanded the surrender of trapped Confederate troops. He was in command of the army by April 1862 and fought the bloodiest battle of the war at Shiloh. Grant was given command of the

Department of Tennessee in October 1862 and launched his assaults on Vicksburg. He took the city and was promoted to major general and subsequently fought the Battles of Chickamauga, Chattanooga, Lookout Mountain and Missionary Ridge. Soon after he was promoted to lieutenant general and now commanded all Union armies. He accompanied Meade to fight the Wilderness Campaign, Spotsylvania and Cold Harbor, where casualties earned him the new nickname of 'Butcher Grant'. In June 1864 he attached himself to the Army of the Potomac, remaining with it until April 1865. Sheridan's victory at Five Forks on 1 April 1865 forced Lee to abandon Richmond and Petersburg and Grant was there to cut off Lee's retreat. It was by mutual agreement that the Army of Northern Virginia finally surrendered to Grant at Appomattox Courthouse. After the war Grant became a full general in 1866, and two years later stood as Republican candidate for president and won. He surrounded himself with friends and was not considered to be a successful president, but was nevertheless re-elected in 1872. He left office in 1877 and travelled around the world for two years, returning home short of money. He was forced to sell off his wartime memorabilia and was declared bankrupt in 1884. By now, he was suffering from throat cancer: he died in July 1885 in New York and his remains lie in a mausoleum in the city.

move steadily down the Tennessee river and take on whatever the Confederates chose to offer him.

Grant's next major battle is known either as Pittsburg Landing or Shiloh. He was peacefully eating his breakfast on the morning of 6 April 1862, when he heard heavy firing. He hastened to Pittsburg Landing, 9 miles (15km) away, to find his army under attack. His officers believed that 80,000 Confederates were assaulting their positions, but in truth there was around half this number. But this was counterbalanced by the fact that the Confederates had also overestimated Grant's army, though this had not deterred them from making a concerted attack.

The Confederate offensive consisted of three strong prongs, having the ultimate intention of driving the Union army into the Tennessee river. The Confederate left made impressive progress, but its right and centre met with determined resistance, particularly around the Peach Orchard and the Hornet's Nest. As the Confederate attacks floundered, Grant was able to reorganize and hold the line until darkness fell.

The Confederates lost their able General Albert Sidney Johnston and General Beauregard took over control of the army. On the morning of 7 April Grant threw fresh reserves into the battle, while General Buell held the left and General Lew Wallis the right. As soon as Buell's counter-attack got underway, Sherman's forces in the centre moved forward, regaining the Peach Orchard and the Hornet's Nest. Beauregard's reserves were too late to help him and he decided to withdraw, taking with him 3,000 captured Union soldiers and 30 Union artillery pieces. Total Confederate casualties amounted to 1,728 killed, 8,012 wounded and 959 captured. The Union losses were 13,047, of which 1,754 had been killed.

Back in April 1861 the Union navy had abandoned the large dockyard facility of Gosport Navy Yard, near Portsmouth. The Confederates were delighted and captured large amounts of weapons and stores. Among the booty was the *Merrimac*, a 3,200-ton ironclad vessel, sporting 40 guns,

which was renamed the *Virginia*. On 8 March 1862 the *Virginia* led an attack on Union warships on the west coast of Hampton Roads, Virginia, near Newport News, and sank several of the wooden warships. On the following day she attacked again, but this time was faced with a similar ironclad, the *Monitor*. It was the first battle

ever to see ironclad warships engaged in a fight with one another, but it ended in stalemate. The *Virginia*'s end would come all too soon.

General McClellan's Union army had occupied the York Peninsula, which meant that both Norfolk and Gosport Navy Yards were vulnerable. The *Virginia* was trapped.

OPPOSITE RIGHT TOP: View of Port Royal, South Carolina. Photograph of the Federal navy and seaborne expeditions against the Atlantic coast of the Confederacy, 1861–62.

OPPOSITE RIGHT BELOW: The Peach Orchard, where action during the Battle of Pittsburg Landing (Shiloh) took place in April 1862.

LEFT: **The Battle of Wilson's Creek** *Lithograph by Kurz & Allison, 1893.*

BELOW: The crew on the deck of the **Monitor***.*

Farragut's Fleet Passing Fort Jackson and Fort St. Philip, 1862
J. Joffray (fl.1862).
Oil on canvas.
Chicago Historical Museum, Chicago.

RIGHT: The USS Monitor *and* Canonicus *photographed in the James river, Virginia.*

BELOW: **The First Encounter of Ironclads: Terrific Engagement between the Merrimac and the Monitor, 9 March 1862** *Calvert Lithographing Co., Detroit, Michigan.*

OPPOSITE LEFT: Admiral Farragut of the Union Fleet.

OPPOSITE BELOW: Ruins of Fort Moultrie in Charleston Harbour.

She could not risk the open seas, nor could she risk running aground close to Union batteries. On 10 May her crew set her on fire and at 0500 the following day she blew up. The Union *Monitor* would not last very long either. She sank at midnight on 31 December 1862, under tow into Charleston harbour.

Naval forces were an important aspect of the war. Not only did the Union navy have the job of blockading the South, it was also key in supporting army operations. By December 1863 Lincoln could report that the Union navy had a strength of 588 vessels, of which 75 were either ironclads or armoured steamers.

A prime example of the importance of naval power was the struggle for the control of the Mississippi river. The Confederates were busy at work, fortifying points along the river to deny control of it to the Union. Most notable was Ship Island, which was 10 miles (16km) off the coast and 60 miles (100km) from both New Orleans and Mobile. In its struggle for control of the

entrance to the Mississippi (St. Philip and Jackson), and then hold the waterway.

Union forces began assembling at Ship Island in February 1862, and the attack was launched the following April. Mortar ships opened fire on the two forts on 18 April, firing a staggering 240 shells per hour. Despite the devastating firepower the forts held on. On 24 April the Union fleet, under Farragut, moved in closer to engage the forts' batteries. The attack worked and despite the determined Confederate defence, New Orleans fell to the Union army.

New Orleans was put under the direct rule of General Benjamin Butler, who imposed a harsh regime on the inhabitants of the city. Among his requirements was the surrender of all firearms. Men were required to take the Oath of Allegiance to the United States, otherwise they would have to pay a fine or be exiled. Butler would remain in post until 24 December 1862, when he returned to active service.

Meanwhile, the Peninsula Campaign had been under way since April 1862. General McClellan first moved against the Confederate-held Yorktown, defended by

river, the Union fixed on Ship Island as its first target, seizing control of the island in September 1861. New Orleans was an important trading port and the Confederates were building warships in the harbour. Logically, the Union needed to take the city, destroy the Confederate forts protecting the

JAMES EWELL BROWN STUART (1833-64)

Stuart was born in Patrick County, Virginia, the son of a lawyer and soldier who had fought in the War of 1812. Stuart graduated thirteenth in his class at West Point in 1854. He saw service in Texas during the Indian Wars and was later transferred as a cavalry officer to Fort Leavenworth. He accompanied Lee in the capture of John Brown at Harper's Ferry in 1859. Stuart was a captain by April 1861 but resigned his commission. The following month he became a lieutenant colonel in the Confederate army and was ordered to Harper's Ferry to join up with Jackson. After service in the Shenandoah Valley he fought at Bull Run in July 1861, and two months later was promoted to brigadier general, fighting the Battles of Yorktown and Williamsburg in the Peninsula. As a consummate cavalry commander he was invaluable to Lee during the Seven Days' Battles and at Second Bull Run in August 1862. After the battles of Antietam and Fredericksburg he took over Stonewall Jackson's corps, and in June 1863 fought the inconclusive battle at Brandy Station. He was criticized for not arriving until the second day of the Battle of Gettysburg. During the Wilderness Campaign of 1864 he stopped Union troops at Yellow Tavern, en route to Richmond, but was wounded and died on 12 May 1864. Lee missed him greatly for his constant protection from unexpected attacks by the Union forces.

The Monitor and the Merrimac, the First Fight between Ironclads in 1862
From a lithograph by Julian Oliver Davidson (1853–94), published in 1886 by Louis Prang & Company.
Private collection.

THE CIVIL WAR

15,000 men, having at his disposal upwards of 100,000 men and 44 batteries of artillery. In the first skirmish of the campaign at Lee's Mill (16 April) it was the Union that came off second best.

Facing McClellan was General Joseph E. Johnston, who proposed to abandon Yorktown and concentrate a powerful force near Richmond, which had been the strategy that had led to the abandonment of Gosport Navy Yard. McClellan sent off troops in pursuit of the retreating Confederates on 4 May and they followed the road from Yorktown to Williamsburg, clashing late that night and during the following day. It was the first of a series of inconclusive engagements. McClellan had managed to convince himself that he was facing a force much larger than his own. He demanded reinforcements and consequently, by the end of May, his own army numbered 127,166, supported by another 14,007 men under General Wool.

On 27 May McClellan attacked a Confederate force of some 9,000 that was protecting the Virginia Central Railroad. The Union army scored a decisive victory, but to stop McClellan from seizing the initiative, the Confederates launched a counter-attack on 31 May, which was beset with problems, mainly due to floodwater. The Battle of Seven Pines saw the Union corps of Keyes and Heintzelman pushed

The Mississippi Delta today. Mississippi was the second state to secede from the Union in January 1861, when it joined six other Cotton States to form the Confederate States of America. Mississippi's position along the lengthy Mississippi river made it strategically important to both the North and South, and dozens of battles were fought near key towns and cities.

General Benjamin F. Butler.

Gun and Mortar Boats on the Mississippi
William Torgerson (fl.1873–1890).
Oil on canvas.
Chicago Historical Museum, Chicago.

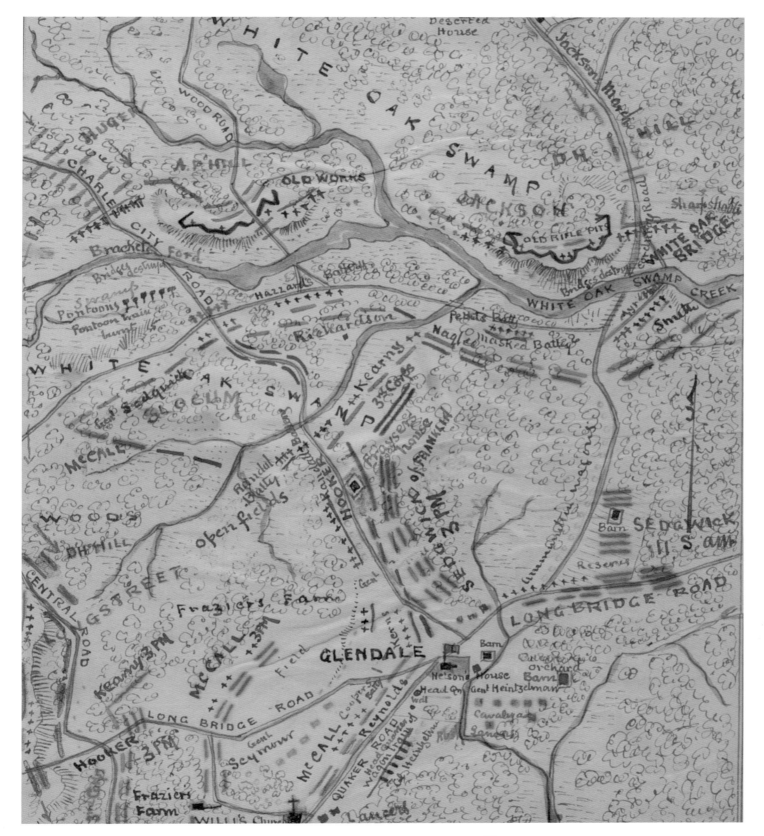

OPPOSITE: *White Oak Swamp, Henrico County, Virginia.*

LEFT: *Position of the Union Army on 30th June 1862, illustrating the Battle of Frayser's (Frazier's) Farm, one of the Seven Days' Battles, which began on 26 June and ended on 1 July 1862, and marked the culmination of the Peninsula Campaign.*

RIGHT: The Battle of Seven Pines (Battle of Fair Oaks), fought from 31 May–1 June 1862, was part of the Peninsula Campaign. A 32–pdr. field howitzer is pictured in the foreground.

BELOW: The Fair Oaks battle site.

BELOW RIGHT: General John Ellis Wool.

Lee to take over from Johnston. Lee received reinforcements and was determined to attack McClellan and force his army away from Richmond.

First he reinforced General Jackson in the Shenandoah Valley. Jackson would be vital in his own offensive, and would strike at the Union right, then Lee's main force would hit Mechanicsville and fight towards Gaines' Mill. He proposed to hit McClellan on 26 June. Lee's offensive sparked off what became known as the Seven Days' Battles (25 June–1 July 1862). On 26 June the armies clashed at Mechanicsville, on 27 June at Gaines' Mill, at Peach Orchard and Savage's Station on June 29, at Frayser's Farm (Glendale) on June 30 and at Malvern Hill on July 1.

In all, some 91,169 Union troops were engaged, of which 1,734 were killed, 8,062 wounded and 6,053 were posted missing. Lee's Confederates amounted to some 75,769 (other accounts say 95,481), of which 3,478 were killed, 16,261 were wounded and 875 were posted missing.

Despite the casualties, it was McClellan who was in retreat, heading for Harrison's Landing, near the James river, his campaign in the Peninsula now at an end, having lost 15,249 dead, wounded or missing. The Confederates had taken over 10,000

back. Men fought in water up to their knees and many of the wounded were drowned.

Another battle took place on the same day at Fair Oaks Station, in which fighting was so intense that the opposing sides resorted to bayonet attacks. The Confederates were on the verge of a great victory, but Johnston had been badly wounded and the opportunity was lost. This brought about the appointment of Robert E.

prisoners, captured 52 guns and 35,000 muskets and pistols.

General Pope assumed command of a new force called the Army of Virginia on 26 June 1862, his Union army first pushing towards Gordonsville. Lee, meanwhile, confident that McClellan's army held no threat, had despatched Jackson and Ewell to Gordonsville on 13 July, with Pope becoming aware of the Confederate movement on 8 August. Late the next day Union troops moved to within 2 miles (3km) of Cedar Mountain (Slaughter Mountain), where they were engaged by the forward elements of the Confederate army. The outnumbered Union troops first pushed forward, but were then checked and pushed back. Total Union losses amounted to nearly 2,500, whereas the Confederates lost 1,300 men.

ABOVE LEFT: Fair Oaks, Virginia. The old frame house on the battle site was used by Hooker's division as a hospital.

ABOVE: The ruins of Gaines' Mill, in the vicinity of Cold Harbor, during the Peninsula Campaign, fought between April and July 1862, in which the Union failed to capture Richmond, Virginia.

LEFT: Savage's Station served as a Union field hospital after the battle of 29 June 1862.

THE CIVIL WAR

Battle of Williamsburg, 5 May 1862
American School (19th Century).
Lithograph by Kurz & Allison.
Private Collection.

With more Union forces arriving, the Confederates fell back across the Rapidan river. Lee was planning another offensive, but Union cavalry captured his orders on 16 August. Pope knew he could not count on McClellan's help and that the full force of Lee's army would soon strike his own men. Lee pressed on with his audacious attack. Jackson, supported by Stuart's cavalry, covered 51 miles (82km) in two days to reach Bristoe Station on 27 August. Jackson aimed to capture the considerable amount of Union stores held at Manassas Junction.

After a series of skirmishes, Pope abandoned his defensive line and on the same day headed for Manassas Junction, by way of Gainesville, while part of his army clashed with Ewell at Kettle Run, near Bristoe Station. Pope determined to concentrate his army at Manassas Junction and then destroy Jackson before Ewell could support him. Meanwhile, Lee was following the same route Jackson had taken and was closing in on Pope.

The Second Battle of Bull Run (or Manassas) got underway on Friday 29 August 1862. Fighting was severe but by the end of the first day Pope thought he had

ABOVE: Pontoon bridge across the James river.

RIGHT: Cedar Mountain (Slaughter's Mountain), the site of the battle of 9 August 1862. A Confederate battery was sited near Parson Slaughter's house in 1862.

OPPOSITE: Burnside's Bridge was the controversial means by which General Ambrose Burnside and his troops crossed Antietam Creek during the Battle of Antietam.

THE CIVIL WAR

beaten Lee. Pope reported losses of 8,000 and told Washington that Lee had lost twice that number and was in full retreat. He was wrong. Lee attacked the next day and Pope's weary men withdrew. Union losses amounted to 14,462, while the Confederates lost 9,474 men. Pope had missed a golden opportunity to destroy Lee and was forced to resign.

McClellan, despite everything, once again took control of the Union army. He knew that Lee would aim for Maryland and Pennsylvania now that the Peninsula was free of Union troops and Richmond was no longer under threat. On 8 September Lee issued a proclamation to Maryland, begging it to join the Confederacy and promising that his army would come and protect the state. The Confederate army began to move on 12 September. The following day Lee learned that a large Union army was at South Mountain; this was a matter of concern, for at this point his army was split into three moving columns.

Jackson had headed for Harper's Ferry, which he seized, taking 12,000 prisoners,

ABOVE: Soldiers photographed during the Second Battle of Bull Run (Second Battle of Manassas), 29–30 August 1862.

RIGHT: Manassas Junction: damaged rolling stock belonging to the Orange & Alexandria Railroad.

while Longstreet was at Hagerstown and Hill was 13 miles (21km) away at Boonsboro'. Lee had not counted on McClellan moving to stop him, but the Union general had come into possession of one of Lee's orders, showing the routes that would be taken by his troops. McClellan took the order at face value and realized he had a chance to destroy the Confederate army piecemeal.

On 14 September Union troops tried to force the passes around South Mountain, but met with mixed results. Around 28,000 Union troops were involved, facing 18,000 Confederates. By 2000 Lee was convinced his plan was compromised and that the army should retreat to Sharpsburg before proceeding across the Potomac river. There were simply too many risks in trying to remain on the offensive.

Union troops marched through South

ABOVE LEFT: Monument to the Battles of Bull Run.

ABOVE: The remains of a house after battle, Bull Run.

LEFT: Antietam Creek, Maryland.

PAGE 82: Harper's Ferry, Maryland.

IRVIN MCDOWELL (1818–85)

Born in Ohio, McDowell was educated in France before entering West Point, graduating in 1838. For a time he served as a tactics instructor at West Point before seeing active service during the Mexican War. At the outbreak of the American Civil War he was promoted to the rank of brigadier general, charged with protecting Washington. He singularly failed in this role, when he was decisively defeated at the First Bull Run in July 1861 and was replaced by McClellan. McDowell was eventually given command of the 1st corps of the Army of the Potomac and later served under Pope in the newly organized Army of Virginia. He was blamed for the Union failure at Second Bull Run, but was lauded and promoted for his actions at Cedar Mountain. After these two battles, however, he saw no further action and was given the post of Commander of the Pacific Coast. He was promoted to major general in 1865 and was mustered out in September the following year. He continued to serve in the regular army as a major general until his retirement in 1882, but died in San Francisco, California, three years later.

JACKSON, THOMAS JONATHAN 'STONEWALL' (1824–63)
Jackson was born at Clarksburg, West Virginia, and was only two when his father died of typhoid. Jackson entered West Point in 1842, graduating seventeenth out of fifty-nine in 1846. He served in the Mexican War, receiving commendations and promotions for his gallantry, and ended the war as a major. Jackson resigned from the army in 1851 to teach at the Virginia Military Institute in Lexington. In 1859 he was the academy's representative at the execution of the abolitionist, John Brown, where he stood guard. In June 1861 Jackson became a brigadier general in the Confederate army, taking command of the Confederates in the Shenandoah Valley the following October. During the summer of 1862 he won several victories against the Union army before joining Lee in East Virginia. With Lee, he fought in the Seven Days' Battles, and at the Battles of Cedar Mountain, Second Bull Run and Antietam. In October 1862 he became a lieutenant general and was now in command of half the Army of Northern Virginia. He wintered at Chancellorsville and was unfortunately shot by one of his own troops on the evening of 2 May 1863, which led to his arm being amputated. Unfortunately, he developed pneumonia and died on 10 May. Lee said of him '... he has lost his left arm; but I have lost my right arm.'

RIGHT: Harper's Ferry as it appears today.

Mountain, across the valley, and took up positions on the high ground near Antietam Creek. This was a stream with a number of fords and three stone-arched bridges. Lee proposed to make a determined stand at Sharpsburg, just to the west of Antietam Creek.

McClellan had 87,000 men and Lee 59,000, though only 55,000 and 40,000 respectively were engaged. The extremely costly Battle of Antietam got underway on 17 September, with artillery opening fire at dawn; the Union army launched the first assault, with waves of infantry advancing towards the Confederate lines.

LEFT: Harper's Ferry, with a view of the town and railroad bridge, 1862. The town lies where the Potomac and Shenandoah rivers meet.

BELOW: Many old Civil War forts and campsites can be found on Maryland Heights, Harper's Ferry.

ABOVE: General Burnside and his Staff, at Warrenton, Virginia.

ABOVE RIGHT: Brigadier General Joseph Hooker.

RIGHT: Bull Run, view of the battlefield.

One of the most dramatic features of the battle was the crossing of a stone bridge, later dubbed Burnside's Bridge. General Burnside's Union troops tried to force the bridge three times, the assaults taking place between 1000 and 1300, when he eventually succeeded. The assaults cost one of Burnside's brigades along with some 463 casualties.

By nightfall both sides were exhausted. The heavy losses, around 11,500 for each army, blunted Lee's plans, but McClellan failed to follow up and was content to concentrate on reorganizing his forces.

Frustrated by the lack of action, Lincoln demanded that McClellan cross the Potomac river and drive Lee south. McClellan still held back, missing the chance to intercept Lee en route to Richmond. Lee had not been idle; he ordered J.E.B. Stuart, his cavalry commander, to raid Pennsylvania. Stuart started out on 9 October and despite being pursued was able to capture 1,200 horses and take 30 hostages before returning to Virginia.

Burnside assumed control of the Army of the Potomac on 7 November 1862 – once

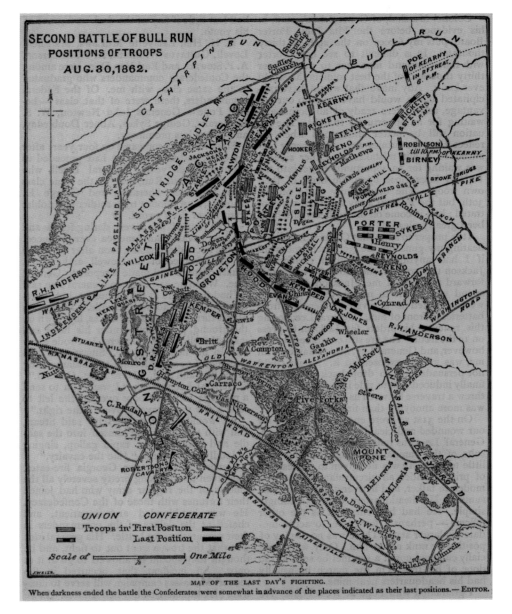

SECOND BATTLE OF BULL RUN
POSITIONS OF TROOPS
AUG. 30, 1862.

UNION   CONFEDERATE
Troops in First Position
Last Position

Scale of _____ One Mile

MAP OF THE LAST DAY'S FIGHTING. —
When darkness ended the battle the Confederates were somewhat in advance of the places indicated as their last positions. — EDITOR.

had 113,000 men, but at Fredericksburg he had lost 12,500. Lee's Confederates amounted to 72,497 directly engaged and they had suffered losses of 5,322. Burnside desperately wanted to attack again, but needed to regroup. It took him until 20 January 1863 to be ready, but by then heavy rains and mud impeded his chances of forcing a battle. Lincoln had seen enough and replaced Burnside with Joseph Hooker.

'Fighting Joe' Hooker took control of the Army of the Potomac on 25 January 1863. He realized that one of the main problems so far was that the Union army had never managed to use its manpower advantage and that only parts of the army had fought in each engagement. On paper, Hooker had 130,000 men, and Lee had barely half that number.

Hooker determined not to attack Lee's defensive positions but to outmanoeuvre him. He left a covering force and marched the bulk of his army along the Rappahannock river, crossing it to place

LEFT: Map showing the positions of troops, roads, railroads, towns, rivers, houses, names of residents, etc., on 30 August 1862, at the end of the Second Battle of Bull Run.

ABOVE: Sudley Ford, Bull Run.

again McClellan had been replaced. Burnside was a reluctant commander, a strict disciplinarian and a difficult man to please. After yet another reorganization his army started towards Fredericksburg, reaching Falmouth, near Fredericksburg, on 17 November. Lee and his army, meanwhile, reached the heights around Fredericksburg two days later.

Burnside dithered for 20 days, giving Lee the opportunity to dig in and site his artillery ready for an attack. At 0300 on 11 December Confederate signal guns gave

warning that the Union army was on the move. Burnside concentrated his artillery on Fredericksburg itself and Union infantry was used to storm the town. After Fredericksburg fell there was a lull in the fighting until the morning of 13 December, when Union troops assaulted the Confederate line, only to be beaten back by the timely arrival of reinforcements. The leading Union regiments lost around 40 per cent of their strength.

Burnside was unable to dislodge the Confederates, however much he tried. He

the Confederates swept towards Howard's 11th Corps. After an initial firefight, which had caught the Union troops unprepared, many of the Union soldiers fled and only darkness saved Howard's men from complete annihilation. At around 2100, riding to scout the positions of the enemy, Jackson was accidentally shot by some of his own men. He failed to recover from his wounds and died on 10 May.

By now, Lee realized that the Union forces facing his defensive lines near Fredericksburg were depleted, and he could afford to send more troops to attack Hooker. Around 10,000 Confederates were left to man Marye's Heights. The covering Union force attacked under General Sedgwick, who had 23,000 men at his disposal. Sedgwick's men took severe casualties but the Confederate line was turned and the rebel defenders fell back.

On 4 May a determined Confederate counter-attack pushed Sedgwick off Marye's Heights. Sedgwick then received an order from Hooker to pull back, but at 0915 Hooker was wounded at Chancellor House. His orders to his subordinates were to withdraw and to protect Washington.

Union losses were around 16,000, around a quarter of them now prisoners,

ABOVE: Catharpin Run, Sudley Church, and the remains of the Sudley Sulphur Spring, Bull Run.

RIGHT: Soldiers relaxing at Brandy Station, Virginia. The Battle of Brandy Station was fought on 9 June 1863, at the start of the Gettysburg Campaign.

OPPOSITE ABOVE LEFT: Fortifications outside Fredericksburg.

OPPOSITE BELOW LEFT: The North Anna bridge after it had been destroyed, Fredericksburg.

OPPOSITE RIGHT: Stone wall along the Sunken Road, Fredericksburg, where a Civil War battle was fought on 13 December 1862.

himself behind the Confederate line. Hooker sent his cavalry, under Stoneman, to cut off Lee's supply lines to Richmond. Stoneman began his raid on 29 April 1863. Meanwhile the main Union army was around Chancellorsville.

On the following day Hooker pushed his men up the Orange Turnpike from Chancellorsville to Fredericksburg, meeting with determined resistance. With his lead elements in retreat, Hooker set up defensive positions around Chancellorsville. Meanwhile, Confederate cavalry commander J.E.B. Stuart discovered that Hooker's right flank was unprotected and Lee immediately ordered Stonewall Jackson to lead his 28,000-man corps to attack it.

Jackson's troops collided with the Union General Howard's corps at Dowdall's Tavern. It was now the afternoon of 2 May 1863. Emerging from the woodland tracks

BULL RUN TO GETTYSBURG

**The Battle of Chancellorsville,
Virginia, 30 April– 6 May 1863**
The American School.
Lithograph.
Newberry Library, Chicago, Illinois.

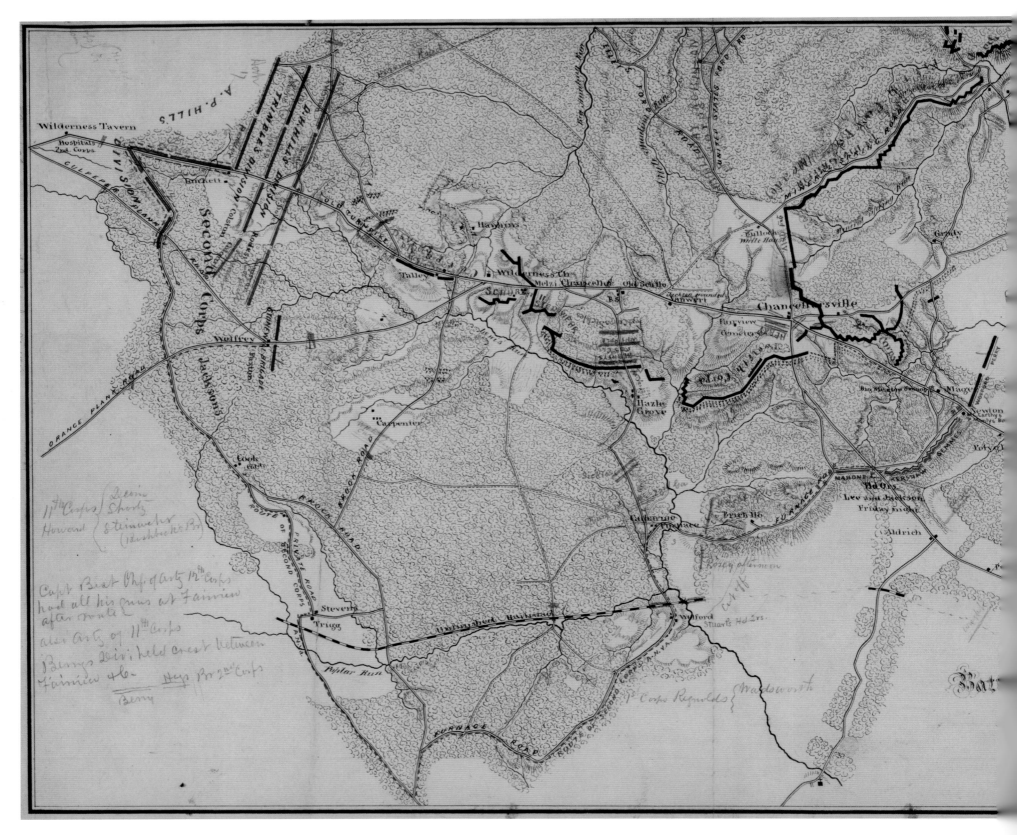

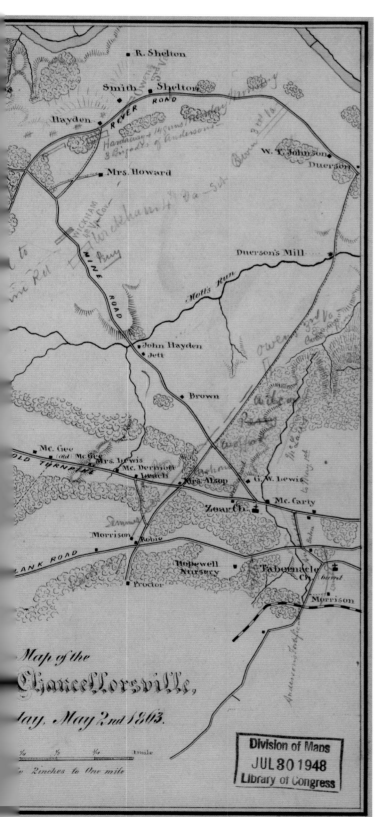

OPPOSITE: *Map of the Battle of Chancellorsville.*

ABOVE: *Ruins of a house at Chancellorsville.*

LEFT: *The Rappahannock river and Germanna Ford.*

Marye's Heights National Cemetery, Fredericksburg, where 15,000 Union soldiers are buried.

while Confederate losses were around 12,827. Now Hooker had missed a great chance; he had been indecisive and, had he reinforced Howard when Jackson first attacked, he would have rolled up the Confederate army.

By mid-May 1862 General Henry Halleck had combined the Armies of the Mississippi, Ohio and Tennessee and was pushing towards Corinth. Facing him were Beauregard's 50,000 Confederates, while Halleck could muster 100,000 men.

Memphis had fallen to the Union in July 1862. It was now possible to navigate as far as Confederate-held Vicksburg, but in September 1862 the Confederates had seized Ruka, Mississippi, and in early October had attacked Corinth.

Grant proposed to move on Vicksburg, but it would be a tough assignment. The United States Navy commander, Farragut, had first called on Vicksburg to surrender in May 1862. He could not press his point, however, because he was not strong enough to duel with the batteries defending the city. Grant now proposed to disembark his army just below Vicksburg, covered by the navy. Consequently, on 16 April 1863 the navy started out and began to engage the Confederate batteries that night. Meanwhile, Grant's troops landed ready for an assault

FAR LEFT: Major General Henry W. Halleck.

ABOVE: Wounded Indian sharpshooters on Marye's Heights.

LEFT: **Battle of Corinth, Mississippi, 3–4 October 1862**
Lithograph by Kurz & Allen, 1891

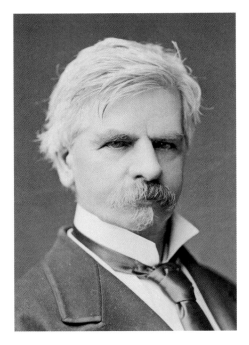

WILLIAM TECUMSEH SHERMAN (1820–91)

Sherman was born at Lancaster, Ohio, in 1820, but his father, a lawyer, died when his son was only nine. He attended West Point military academy, where he graduated sixth in 1840. He was later regarded as something of an eccentric, but he was a tenacious fighter and ruthless leader, especially in the latter stages of the American Civil War. He was at the First Battle of Bull Run in 1861, where he commanded a brigade of volunteers, after which he was promoted to brigadier general and sent to Kentucky as deputy commander of the Department of the Cumberland, under Robert Anderson, the hero of Fort Sumter, whom he later succeeded. He served under General Ulysses S. Grant in 1862 and 1863 during the campaigns that led to the fall of the Confederate stronghold of Vicksburg on the Mississippi river, and which culminated in the defeat of the Confederate armies in the state of Tennessee. In 1864, Sherman succeeded Grant as Union commander in the Western Theatre of war. He proceeded to capture the city of Atlanta, a military success that contributed decisively to the re-election of Abraham Lincoln as president. Sherman's famous 'March to the Sea', through Georgia and the Carolinas, further undermined the Confederates, and he accepted the surrender of all the Confederate armies in the Carolinas, Georgia, and Florida in April 1865. After the civil war, Sherman replaced Grant as Commanding General of the Army (1869–83), and as such, was responsible for the conduct of the Indian Wars in the Western United States. He steadfastly refused to be drawn into politics and in 1875 published his memoirs, one of the most vivid accounts of the American Civil War. He retired in February 1884 and died in New York in 1891.

on the city. Elements of Grant's force, under Sherman, marched cross-country and attacked Confederate towns as far as Jackson on the Pearl river. Grant's men slowly advanced on Vicksburg, expecting a major fight to wrest the city from the Confederacy.

Facing Grant was General Pemberton, who by 1 July realized that unless he got help very soon, Vicksburg was doomed. Lee could not afford to detach men from his army and consequently a white flag was raised over Vicksburg on 3 July. The following day Pemberton's garrison of 30,000 men surrendered.

By 9 July Grant was at Jackson, chasing General Johnston's army of 22,000 men. Johnston was determined not to yield any

JOSEPH HOOKER (1814–79)
Hooker was born in Massachusetts and graduated from West Point before serving in the Seminole and Mexican Wars. He became involved in fierce disputes with General Winfield Scott, which led him to resign from the army, and he was not recalled until August 1861. He was a heavy drinker and was disagreeable and aggressive, which earned him his nickname 'Fighting Joe'. Hooker was promoted to the rank of major general and fought at the Battle of Seven Pines and in the Seven Days' Battles, and served under Pope at the Second Bull Run, Antietam and Fredericksburg. He became commander of the Army of the Potomac, relieving Burnside of the position, but lost his first battle at Chancellorsville and was replaced by Meade. From then on Hooker served in support roles, but took Lookout Mountain and Missionary Ridge. He was mustered out in 1866 but two years later suffered a stroke. Hooker's name is forever linked with the nickname given to the prostitutes that followed his army and he is often described as having been immodest and immoral. He died in Long Island, New York, in October 1879 and was buried in Cincinnati.

further ground. He repulsed a Union attack on 12 July, but withdrew four days later.

That same day Port Hudson, Louisiana, some 135 miles (217km) upriver from New Orleans, fell to Union forces. It had had a large garrison but this had been stripped to support Vicksburg. Facing the 7,000 defenders were 20,000 Union troops under General Banks. After a stiff fight the Confederates surrendered and 6,000 prisoners were taken. This is of great significance to African-Americans as it was the first battle to see black troops of the Corps D'Afrique within the Union ranks.

Back in Virginia in the spring of 1863 Lee had been charged with the task of bringing the war to the North. He was confident that Richmond was not under threat and proposed to strike deep into

OPPOSITE TOP LEFT: General John Clifford Pemberton.

OPPOSITE TOP RIGHT: General Nathaniel Prentice Banks.

OPPOSITE BELOW: **The Siege of Vicksburg, 1863**
Lithograph by Kurz & Allison, 1888

LEFT: The Vicksburg battleground, Louisiana.

JOHN BELL HOOD (1831–79)

Hood was born in Owingsville, Kentucky, in June 1831, and acquired a place at West Point through his uncle, a member of the U.S. House of Representatives. He was constantly in trouble, due to his appearance, behaviour and occasional disobedience, and graduated close to the bottom of his class in 1853. After frontier service in Texas in the 1850s, he joined the Confederates in Virginia in April 1861, becoming first a colonel and then a brigadier general by March 1862. Hood had a reputation for hard fighting and reckless courage. He was involved in dozens of battles, including Williamsburg, Seven Pines, Gaines' Mill, Thoroughfare Gap, Second Bull Run and South Mountain. He distinguished himself at Fredericksburg in December 1862 and led a division at Gettysburg in July 1863, where he was badly wounded. Hood commanded a corps at Chickamauga, when he was again wounded, which led to his leg being amputated. After convalescing at Richmond, Hood was given another corps in July 1864. He lost the Battle of Peachtree Creek that month but managed to hold Sherman off at Atlanta for a short time. Hood's troops retreated to the Ohio Valley, where he faced his former tutor, George Thomas. Thomas forced Hood to retreat into Mississippi, where he gave up his command in July 1865. Hood surrendered in May 1865 and settled down as a businessman in New Orleans after the war. Both he and his wife died of yellow fever in August 1879, leaving behind ten orphaned children.

Pennsylvania. After reorganizing the Army of Northern Virginia he set out, leaving a shadow force to watch Hooker's army. By early June there were scattered reports of large columns of Confederate infantry in the Shenandoah Valley, heading north.

On 28 June 1863 the Army of the Potomac had yet another commander, when General George Meade, who faced a baptism of fire, replaced Hooker. He needed to reorganize, then find Lee and beat him. The Confederates had learned that the Army of the Potomac was on the move, and Lee was concerned that the Union army would get behind him and cut him off. He ordered his troops to concentrate around Carlisle and Gettysburg.

Early on the morning of 1 July, Lee rode from his headquarters at Greenwood, along the Chambersburg Pike, towards Gettysburg. He had barely begun his ride when he heard artillery fire. Running north-east from Gettysburg was the road to Philadelphia, to the north Carlisle was 27 miles (43km) away, while to the south-west the road ran to Hagerstown, barely 6 miles (10km) distant.

Meade had given control of three corps of infantry and cavalry to General John Reynolds, who was certain that a battle was imminent and had taken up position on the

Emmitsburg Road, close to Marsh Creek. He had cavalry watching Gettysburg under Buford.

The first Confederate troops appeared early on 1 July, approaching Gettysburg, but dismounted Union cavalry held them off. Reynolds and Buford quickly realized the seriousness of the situation and Reynolds ordered his corps to march on Gettysburg. Both sides poured men into the battle and by mid-afternoon the Union forces had fallen back to a defensive line along Cemetery Hill. With more troops arriving, darkness fell, and it was necessary to

OPPOSITE ABOVE: Big Round Top, Gettysburg, Pennsylvania.

OPPOSITE BELOW: Little Round Top, Gettysburg.

ABOVE LEFT: Three Confederate prisoners, Gettysburg.

LEFT: Battery B, Second U.S. Artillery.

TOP: Cemetery Hill, Gettysburg.

ABOVE: Federal breastworks on Culp's Hill, Gettysburg.

The Battle of Gettysburg, 1863
Sebastian Mayer (19th century).
Oil on canvas.
David David Gallery, Philadelphia.

RIGHT: Headquarters of General Lee on the Chambersburg Pike, Gettysburg.

OPPOSITE: Men gathered at Gettysburg for the laying of the cornerstone of the Soldier's National Monument, on the anniversary of Gettysburg in 1865.

PAGE 104: **The Field of Gettysburg, 1–3 July 1863**
Theodore Ditterline.
Lithograph.
Duval & Son 1863.

PAGES 104–105: Gettysburg National Memorial Park, General Oliver Howard's statue on Cemetery Hill.

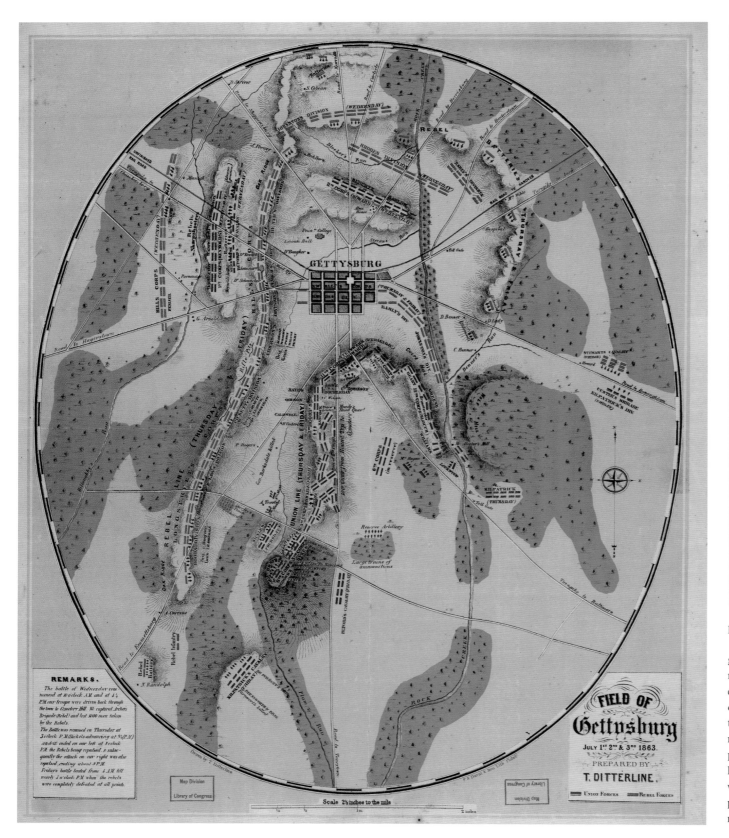

postpone the engagement until morning.

The second day of the battle centred on geographical features that have come to mean much in American history. The extreme left flank of the Union army rested on Big Round Top, Little Round Top and the Devil's Den, and it was here that the main weight of the Confederate attack took place on 2 July. Overshadowed by the gallant heroics of the battlefield in this area, there were also other major fights that day, particularly the Confederate assaults on the right flank of the Union army at Culp's Hill.

GEORGE BRINTON MCCLELLAN (1826–85)

McClellan was born in Philadelphia, Pennsylvania. He graduated from West Point in 1846, where he was second in his class. He served as an engineering officer during the Mexican War, and between 1848 and 1851 taught military engineering at West Point, later becoming Chief Engineer of the Department of Texas. In March 1855 he was assigned to the cavalry, where he developed the famous McClellan Saddle. From 1857 to 1861 he worked as a civilian, having resigned his commission, but he joined the Ohio Volunteers and was given the command of the Department of Ohio. McClellan then took command of the Army of the Potomac but, partly due to illness and dithering, made little progress and was replaced in March 1862. After Pope was defeated at the Second Bull Run in August 1862, McClellan was given command once again, leading his men at South Mountain and at Antietam, but lost command once again in November 1862. He was told to return to New Jersey to await orders, which never came. McClellan stood against Lincoln in the presidential election of 1864 and having failed to beat Lincoln, became New Jersey's governor in the 1870s and 1880s. He died in October 1885 at Orange, New Jersey.

In each case, determined Union defenders met equally determined Confederate assaults.

It was the third day of Gettysburg, 3 July, that lived most vividly in the memory of those who fought in the battle and which captured the imagination of generations thereafter. With Lee rebuffed on the previous day, uncharacteristically he resorted to desperate measures to dislodge the Union army from its defensive positions. General Pickett's three brigades had arrived during the afternoon of 2 July, and his men would lead an attack on the Union centre, supported by attacks on the Union right.

Pickett's 12,500 men (of his total of 15,000), after a two-hour bombardment, charged out of the woods of Seminary Ridge, straight at the area of the Union line in front of Meade's headquarters. Beneath a torrent of fire the Confederates pressed on, the Confederate batteries being unable to assist for fear of hitting their own men. Leading Confederate regiments lost between 50 to 70 per cent of their strength as they ran straight into musket volleys and

THE CIVIL WAR

The Battle of Gettysburg
The American School (19th century).
Lithograph, published c.1863.
Chicago Historical Museum, Chicago.

ABOVE: Devil's Den, Gettysburg.

RIGHT: National memorial with cannon, Gettysburg.

OPPOSITE LEFT: The Gettysburg National Military Park on Oak Ridge.

OPPOSITE RIGHT: Map of the Battle of Gettysburg, showing troop and military positions.

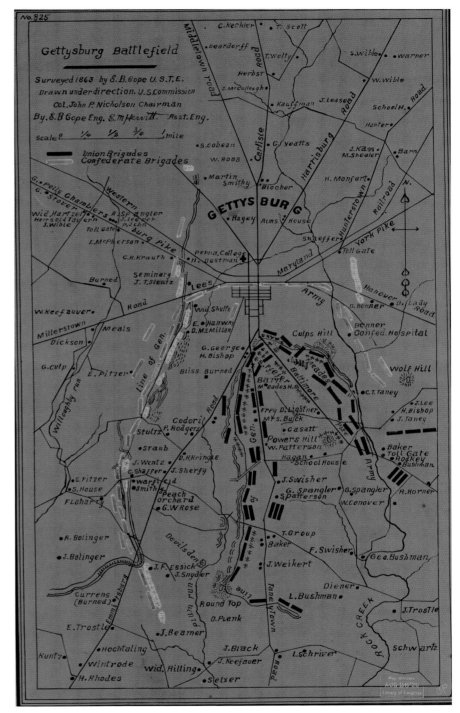

grapeshot. For brief moments the Confederates overran Union artillery batteries, but fresh waves of Union reinforcements beat them back. Some surrendered, others ran back, but the dead and the wounded were predominant in the field.

Lee rode back to console Pickett and his men. It had been a gallant attempt, but in truth Lee realized he had made a serious error of judgement. Pickett told him 'I have no division now.'

Lee took full responsibility for the failure. However, the Union army was in no better shape and could not advance; but Lee and the Army of Northern Virginia had been bested and heavy casualties had been inflicted on the Confederates.

Meade had had 93,500 men engaged in the battle and had lost a staggering 23,003, and Confederate losses were proportionately more grievous. Lee had deployed 75,054 men and had taken 20,451 casualties.

In November 1863 Lincoln visited the battlefield and delivered his famous Gettysburg address: 'The world will little note, nor long remember, what we say here, but it can never forget what they did here. It is for us the living, rather, to be dedicated here to the unfinished work which they who fought here have thus far so nobly advanced. It is rather for us to be here dedicated to the great task remaining before us – that from these honoured dead we take increased devotion to that cause for which they gave their last full measure of devotion.'

Gettysburg saw the last major Confederate attempt to invade the North. Again, the Union army could have finished the war had Meade struck against Lee's crippled army. The Army of the Potomac had suffered defeats at the hands of the Confederates too often, and ditherers had commanded them for too long; now they hoped to enjoy the fruits of a great victory.

Coupled with the loss of Vicksburg, the Battle of Gettysburg saw the high tide of the Confederate successes ebb and flow away. From now on the war would be fought on the Union's terms

RIGHT: **His Army Broke up and**
Followed Him Weeping and Sobbing
(from 'General Lee as I Knew Him',
by A.R.H Ranson).
Painting by Howard Pyle (1853–1911).
Oil on canvas.
Published in Harper's Monthly Magazine,
February 1911.
Delaware Art Museum, Wilmington,
U.S.A./Bequest of Jessie Harrington.

OPPOSITE: **Let Us Have Peace**
by Jean Leon Gerome Ferris (1863–1930).
Private Collection.
The surrender of General Robert E. Lee to
General Grant at Appomattox Courthouse.

POLITICS OF THE NORTH & SOUTH

FAR RIGHT: President Lincoln (left) and General George B. McClellan in the general's tent during the Battle of Antietam in 1862.

BELOW RIGHT: President Abraham Lincoln (1809–65), the 16th president of the United States.

BELOW FAR RIGHT: James Buchanan.

OPPOSITE ABOVE: Band of the 107th U.S. Colored Infantry at Fort Corcoran, Arlington, Virginia.

OPPOSITE: General McClellan and his wife.

Many pondered the question as to why the great democratic institution of the United States appeared to have failed. Ever since the 1820s it seemed as though the more powerful North had been unable to rein in the South. Even bigger federations of states and territories had been able to cope with change far better than the United States; people looked at the Roman and British Empires and wondered why the United States had so singularly failed to remain a cohesive unit. What seemed to be the answer was the fact that most of the rest of the world had abolished slavery, or had at least restricted it, but the United States had expanded it instead. Buchanan's ditherings in the last months of his presidency had not helped; in fact he had failed to act as the Southern states threatened secession before taking the ultimate step. Few truly believed that Abraham Lincoln was up

to the job and many thought he would follow Buchanan in his failure.

In the early months of the Civil War all Lincoln could do was hope the Union would survive. Disastrous defeats piled huge pressure on him as each successive commanding general failed him in the field. But as this was happening, the political system continued to operate. There were congressional, state and local elections in 1862 and a presidential election in 1864. The continuation of politics as usual was vital to the stability of the United States, in that democracy was seen to be still working.

Some Democrats in the North were seen as guilty by association with the secessionists. Many of them harboured hopes that the war

would prove so ruinous for the North that an armistice would take place and a separate Confederacy would co-exist alongside what remained of the Union. For some time they believed that all the Confederacy had to do was endure the war; it would be the North that would capitulate, seeking to end the conflict it was not winning. To this end, every expenditure connected with the war was challenged by the Democrats, in the hope of wearing the Republicans down.

They also challenged arrests of those considered to be disloyal to the Union, the Emancipation Proclamation, and the recruitment of black soldiers from 1862. The Democrats would find an able and vociferous leader in General McClellan, when he was forced out of the army.

Slowly, public opinion began to turn in favour of emancipation and eventually emancipation and Union victory became synonymous, much to the credit of Lincoln. He had held the Republicans together, acted with sensitivity, and had never tried to coerce his colleagues into making decisions they

were not yet ready to contemplate.

When he came to power in 1861 it was clear that he hated slavery, but he was not, as yet, an abolitionist. He believed the Constitution would deal with slavery, by curtailing its spread while working for its extinction. Above all, Lincoln believed that the light but steady hand of Washington would guide the people and the states. He wanted the people to be independent and for the states to be strong, while acting together as a nation. Such was Lincoln's view of democracy that his vision attracted the financial genius of Secretary of the Treasury, Salmon P. Chase, the ultimate administrator, Secretary of War, Edwin M. Stanton, and influential abolitionists such as Frederick Douglass.

Lincoln used to liken his government and army to a wagon with four different teams of horses. In the lead team were the radical Republicans, desperate to gain emancipation and to crush the Confederacy. In the next were the more moderate Republicans, who sometimes sped ahead with the radicals and

at other times stopped altogether. As his government was a coalition, the third contained Democrats, who simply moved towards their goal of a reformed Union with the South. The final team comprised the old-fashioned Democrats, who did everything to hinder the progress of the Union and even reverse its course. Added to these four disparate groups were the Copperheads – extreme anti-war Democrats – who wanted peace on any terms.

The Copperheads were particularly active in Illinois, Indiana and Ohio. Lincoln had his own subtle way of dealing with them: when Clement Vallandigham, an Ohio Congressman, violated a general order forbidding declarations of sympathy towards the Confederacy in 1863, he was arrested and Lincoln banished him from the Union. He was sent through the front lines to the Confederacy and from there to Canada, to return in 1864 with his tail between his legs.

The Republican majority in the House of Representatives was cut from 35 to 18 as a result of the 1862 elections, which did not deter Lincoln from taking the long-term view. He sacked General McClellan and announced a two-part Emancipation Proclamation. The first was that all slaves would be permanently freed in all areas of the Confederacy that had not already returned to Federal control by 1 January 1863. The second part, after the deadline had been passed, was to authorize the Provost Marshall General of the Union army, under the Conscription Act of March 1863, to begin enrolling both black and white men.

Fighting on what appeared to be an anti-war platform, the Democrats, led by the former General McClellan, were crushed by Lincoln in the 1864 presidential election. In fact, Lincoln's share of the popular vote was 15 per cent more than it had been in 1860. He was the first president to have been re-elected since Jackson.

The politics of the Confederate States of America is more difficult to express. There was no long-term vision of the future, since it was their desire to preserve their own way of life, which they regarded as threatened by the dominance of the North and the

government in Washington. The basis upon which they had seceded and fought the Civil War was how they interpreted the contract signed back in 1789. The Federal government formed at that time was intended to secure the interests of the member states, because they felt the Union had failed. Consequently, they felt free to declare the contract void and regain their independence.

The Confederate Constitution was essentially conservationist and nationalistic, which very much reflected the Constitution of the old Union. A Confederate president could serve for six years but not seek re-

election. He could request expenditure, but it would have to be agreed by Congress. On 21 March 1861, Vice President Alexander H. Stephens confirmed that slavery was the 'cornerstone' of the Confederacy.

Jefferson Davis had been chosen as Confederate president for his moderate views, having all the necessary credentials to make him the ideal choice. He was a West Point graduate, a planter, a congressman, a secretary of war and a senator. His major shortcomings were his inability to delegate, his tendency to hold grudges, and his misplaced loyalty to people who were

The Cavalry Charge of Lt. Henry B. Hidden, 1862
Victor Nehlig (1830–1909).
Oil on canvas.
Collection of the New York Historical Society.

BELOW: **The Copperhead Plan for Subjugating the South**
The cartoon shows a delegation of Copperheads entreating a Southerner to return to the Union.

liabilities to the cause. Both Davis and Stephens were selected and inaugurated with indecent speed (two weeks). Davis set about choosing his cabinet, taking men from every original Confederate state. He also built up a selection of advisers, on whose opinion he could rely.

As mobilization got under way, Arkansas, North Carolina, Tennessee and Virginia joined the Confederacy and it seemed for a while that Kentucky, Maryland and Missouri would follow suit. It was decided to reward Virginia for its allegiance to the South by placing the Confederate capital in Richmond.

It soon became clear, however, that the Confederacy needed central control; for example, the states needed to hang on to their militia troops, rather than releasing them to serve in Confederate freed armies.

From early on it had been obvious that the victories of 1861 would not be enough to defeat the Union. Davis and the Confederacy had hoped for a short, decisive war, but the Union was in for the longer haul. Moreover, it had access to greater resources and could strike anywhere. In the spring of 1862 Davis decided he would declare martial law, suspend trial by jury, and introduce conscription. Congress complied.

The situation was dangerous. A large Union army was rampaging through Tennessee and the Army of the Potomac was advancing upon Richmond. In the summer, under the command of Lee, the Confederates had driven the Union army out and had invaded Maryland, while in the West Bragg had invaded Kentucky. The work of Davis and his cabinet seemed to be satisfactory.

The winter of 1862 was harsh for the South, and the inadequacies of its infrastructure led to food shortages, while cotton could not be exported because of the Union blockades.

By March 1863 the military had been empowered to seize private property for repayment at fixed prices. Inflation was running away unchecked, tax had increased, and when the South lost at Gettysburg and Vicksburg, it looked as though all the sacrifices had been for nothing. By the

LEFT: Officers of the Army of the Potomac in their winter quarters at Brandy Station.

BELOW: Jefferson Davis and his Cabinet.

PAGES 120–121: **Civil War Engagement, 1865**
Xanthus Russell Smith (1839–1929).
Oil on canvas.
Private Collection.

autumn of 1864 the Confederacy was all but bankrupt. As Vice President Stephens remarked: 'What good is independence, if the South must sell its very soul to secure it?' Lee had been pushed back to Richmond and Petersburg, Sherman was in the Carolinas, chasing the Confederates, and all that was left by way of assets were the slaves.

On 7 November 1864 Davis asked Congress for the money to purchase 40,000 slaves, proposing to use them in a non-combatant role within the army, after which time they would be given their freedom. This was the first, very belated step towards Southern emancipation, and both Davis and Robert E. Lee were convinced that salvation for the South lay in taking this course. Congress thought they meant slave soldiers, but Davis wrote emancipation into the orders implementing the law.

So clearly slavery in the South had run its course – brought to an end by an absolute need. The Confederacy lasted a while into 1865; Davis fled from Richmond on 2 April and kept on running when he heard of Lee and Johnston's surrenders. He still hoped to defy Lincoln and Washington, and still harboured desires to lead an insurgent force against the Union. But the South would no longer oblige; it had had enough.

Davis was finally captured at Irwinville, Georgia, on 10 May 1865, by a detachment of Union cavalry. The Confederate States of America had lost their first and only president.

CHAPTER SIX
BEHIND THE LINES

RIGHT and BELOW: Camp of the 50th Regiment, Pennsylvania Infantry, at Gettysburg.

Even though daily life in the North had been hardly touched by the war, there was no initial shortage of recruits for the Union army. There had been an enormous surge of patriotism and Lincoln's original call for 75,000 volunteers had been far exceeded by overzealous state governors. In fact, the Union had suffered something of a crisis, its army support systems being woefully inadequate; on the one hand it had a surfeit of volunteers, but on the other, there was a lack of uniforms, equipment and boots. In storage were some 300,000 muskets, but most of them were obsolete models, often as much as 50 years old.

However, the initial wave of patriotism soon faltered, when it was realized that the War Department was unable to ensure its

soldiers were properly fed. Soldiers' Aid associations sprang up to collect supplies and distribute them to the troops, but this was never going to be a long-term solution. All was chaos and Washington seemed unable to suggest a viable way forward. Matters became even more serious after 3 May 1861, when Lincoln asked for an additional 42,000 men, expecting them to serve for three years.

By now the state arsenals were empty, rifles and muskets were hard to come by and they were expensive to buy. The arms manufacturers in the North could produce no more than around 5,000 weapons per month, and the North needed ten times as many.

The situation was no better in the South and gradually both Union and Confederate purchasing agents began to travel the world, looking for new sources of weapons. They were able to buy freely from both the British

THE CIVIL WAR

and the French, but these new weapons would take time to manufacture and ship to the United States. As an interim measure, weapons that had been superseded by new issues were brought out of mothballs by the Belgians, the Prussians and the Austrians. The Confederacy would continue to rely on imported firearms, but by the spring of 1862 manufacturers in the North had stepped up production and were able to fulfil demand.

It was not only the infantry that suffered from a lack of supply. Although the South had plentiful equipment for its horses, so that it could easily form cavalry and artillery regiments, what was lacking on both sides were carbines, revolvers and sabres. The states each had complements of artillery pieces, so for the most part, supply of these weapons was not a general concern.

The Confederacy would, however, suffer from a distinct lack of horses, particularly after traditional horse-rearing areas had

William T. Sherman at Federal Fort No. 7, Atlanta, Georgia, September–November, 1864. Photographed by George N. Barnard, who produced the best documentary record of the war in the West.

THE CIVIL WAR

fallen to Union forces. Thereafter, any available horse was pressed into action.

Both the Union and the Confederacy needed to ensure a steady supply of new recruits for their armies. Mass rallies were held and the Union offered bounties as rewards. The problem, as in most wars, was that civilian wages had increased, due primarily to the fact that fewer labourers were now available, which did not make the army or navy particularly strong attractions. Moreover, farms had lost many of their casual labourers and farmers were keen to hold onto their sons. It soon became clear, particularly to the North, that volunteers and drafts alone were not going to supply enough troops; the Confederacy first, and then much later the Union, would have to resort to conscription.

For the North there was the problem of

LEFT: The devastation of war, Charleston, South Carolina.

BELOW LEFT: Ruins of a paper mill in Richmond, Virginia.

BELOW: Buildings destroyed by fire, Richmond.

THE CIVIL WAR

what became known as bounty jumpers. Men would sign up, receive their state and Federal bounties and then promptly desert. Then, under an assumed name, they would present themselves to another recruiting officer, collect the bounties again and move on. There were also those who specialized in substitute brokering, substitutes being acceptable if an individual could find another man willing to take his place. This was a practice found in both the North and the South; once the Union army began to accept black troops, substitute brokers found an almost bottomless pit of potential income.

Conscription was far better organized in the South: after all, there were far fewer men and it was far more difficult to evade the draft. The South, of course, was at a distinct manpower disadvantage, while the North was able to conscript, equip, train and deploy almost a million men over a three-year period. With this enormous army at its disposal, however, the North faced considerable problems in organizing it and making sure the necessary resources were supplied when required.

The South, of course, was far less developed in terms of industry and was highly dependent on imports. Stringent measures were taken to ensure that cash crops, such as cotton, were not grown in preference to food. By 1863 the Confederates had gone as far as demanding that farmers donate ten per cent of all of their food crops to the armed forces, in spite of which there were still enormous shortages. But by 1863, certainly in terms of food, the South had become practically self-sufficient.

Just as Northern civilians did not suffer greatly during the Civil War, with the exception of those affected by occupation, so standards of living were at least stable for a time. But as the war continued, it became increasingly difficult to obtain manufactured goods. Tea and coffee were hard to find, though basic staples, such as pork, bacon, molasses and cornmeal, were always available.

As more men were recruited into the army the shortfall in manpower behind the lines had to be replaced. The old, children and women were therefore obliged to work the farms, particularly in the South, for it should be remembered that the vast majority of the South population did not have slaves of their own.

The centre of the Confederacy was Richmond, a place with industrial capacity and formerly many workers. Due to its geographical location, however, it was becoming increasingly difficult to get supplies into the city, causing the cost of living to rise dramatically, and even prompting bread riots. The Confederacy's paper money became increasingly worthless, as shops and traders began to demand payment in gold or silver, a far more stable form of currency. By 1864 it was not unusual to be paying 1,200 Confederate dollars for a barrel of flour. Shortages hit the South in many different ways, including the restricted printing of newspapers. There, few books were printed, though in the North many newspapers and magazines were published each week.

As for the civilians during the American Civil War, particularly those in remote locations, the carnage of the conflict hardly touched them at all. Increasingly, however, civilians in the South were faced with a total disruption of their way of life as increasingly large numbers of Union troops began to forge deep into the Southern states. Now they could expect their homes to be looted, their possessions stolen or burned, their horses taken and, of course, in relevant cases, their slaves freed. Similar dangers pertained in the border states and the areas through which the armies marched and fought. When Lee launched his invasion of the North, which culminated in Gettysburg in July 1863, his troops, like many, lived off the land and took whatever they could find.

There were other examples of men hell-bent on bringing the war to peaceful civilian communities. Even though William Quantrill was an Ohio schoolteacher, he nevertheless joined the ranks of the Confederacy, recruiting a large contingent of mounted raiders, which included Frank and Jesse James. Quantrill's raiders attacked Union towns and villages, gunning any man down who got in their way, as well as burning and looting. Quantrill's reign of terror came to an

FAR LEFT: **Drummer Boy**
Julian Scott (1846–1901), 1891.
David David Gallery, Philadelphia.

ABOVE: Wounded soldiers at Fredericksburg, during the Battle of the Wilderness, 5–7 May 1864.

ABOVE RIGHT: Haxall's House, which was commandeered as a military hospital after the Battle of White Oak Swamp.

RIGHT: The James brothers, Frank (right) and his younger brother Jesse.

end in May 1865, when at just 27 years of age, he was ambushed by Union cavalry, wounded and later died.

The American Civil War claimed four per cent of the entire American male population. Many of the deaths could have been avoided, had there been better medical facilities or, indeed, the North and South had paid some attention to the care of prisoners-of-war. Andersonville in Georgia was a notorious Confederate prisoner-of-war camp, originally intended to house 10,000 prisoners, but by the summer of 1864 32,000 had been incarcerated, crowded together in squalid conditions. Around 13,000 men alone died due to complete neglect, leading the commander of the prison, Henry Wirtz, to be

charged with murder and hanged on 10 November 1865.

By 1862 the war was costing the North alone $2.5m per day, which necessitated a vast injection of cash into the economy. The Northern economy geared itself to soaking up this surfeit of money; factories built cannons, muskets and engines, while farmers stepped up their production of grain and meat. In fact, farm productivity increased significantly.

The Northern textile industry had been stockpiling raw cotton since before the war, but the demand for uniforms was enormous and even these huge resources had become depleted by 1862, causing many of the mills to close down, and forcing 200,000 people out of work. Unemployment, however, was

of no great concern, because the army was desperate for manpower and every business was losing skilled workers every day to conscription. Many of the manufacturers, however, profited from the shortage of cotton, processing rags and raw wool to make poor-quality uniforms that fell apart within weeks. The North, in particular, imported huge amounts of wool from Britain and Australia and this had developed into a flourishing market by the beginning of 1863. Northern mills had found a new source of raw cotton in India, but were also able to obtain increasing amounts from the Union-occupied Southern states.

Paying for the war proved to be problematical for both the North and the South, neither of them being in favour of

heavy taxation. As far as the Union was concerned, bank loans funded the first year of the war. The North decided to take the dollar off the gold standard and in February 1862 $150m of paper money was made legal tender, though not redeemable for gold or silver. Eventually, the Northern government would circulate $450m in paper money and at one point a dollar was only worth 35 cents-worth of gold.

The Confederates also produced paper money but did not make it legal tender, with the effect that the Confederate dollar was virtually worthless: even when the Union dollar was worth 35 cents, it was still worth eight times that of the Confederate dollar. The overall cost of the war for the South requires two calculations. Firstly the war itself cost upwards of $600m in gold, while, on top of this, the emancipation of the slaves wiped out another $3bn.

ABOVE: Prisoner-of-war camp at Andersonville, Georgia, in 1864. A south-westerly view of the stockade showing the deadline.

LEFT: Reading the death warrant to Henry Wirtz, November 1865, Washington D.C. Wirz was the only Confederate soldier to be executed for war crimes in the aftermath of the Civil War.

PAGE 132: **Holding the Line at All Hazards**
William Gilbert Gaul (1855–1919).
Oil on canvas.
Private Collection.

PAGE 133: **A Break: Playing Cards**
Julian Scott (1846–1901), 1881.
Oil on canvas.
Indianapolis Museum of Art.

133

EMANCIPATION

The American Civil War did not begin as a struggle to end slavery, but as a struggle to preserve the Union. Having said that, it was the most important event in African-American history.

The short-term results of the eventual Union victory meant immediate freedom for upwards of 4 million people, while the egalitarian nature of the 13th and 14th amendments to the Constitution would eventually ensure civil rights for the entire black population of the United States.

The fundamental differences of opinion on the issue of slavery are apparent from a remark made by the Vice President of the Confederate States of America, Alexander H. Stephens, speaking in 1861: 'Our Confederacy is founded on the great truth that slavery – subordination to the superior

race – is [the Negro's] natural and normal condition. Thus, our new government is the first in the history of the world based upon this great physical and moral truth.'

Lincoln had originally found himself in something of a quandary regarding emancipation. He is quoted as saying 'if slavery is not wrong, nothing is wrong', yet his primary aim was to preserve the Union and the Union permitted slavery.

Lincoln faced opinions from every side on the issue of abolition. Ardent abolitionists implored him to use his war powers to end slavery (which he did in the end), but against this was the fear that he would drive the four border slave states into the arms of the Confederacy. There was considerable anti-black feeling in the North, and both old-fashioned Republicans and Democrats were set against abolition. Lincoln knew that if he acted too soon, the

South would fully unite against him, and the North would be divided on the issue, and he could afford neither of these things to happen. In his own words, Lincoln summed up the predicament in which he found himself: 'My paramount object in this struggle is to save the Union, and is not either to save or destroy slavery.' These words were written to the ardent abolitionist, Horace Greeley, in August 1862 and Lincoln went on to say: 'If I could save the Union without freeing any slave I would do it; and if I could save it by freeing all the slaves I would do it; and if I could save it by freeing some and leaving others alone, I would also do that.'

Lincoln was not exactly telling the truth, however. At this stage, he had already decided to make a proclamation of

Emancipation Proclamation
of President Abraham Lincoln, Freeing the Slaves of the United States.

primary reason why Lincoln should endorse the call for abolition: 'Why does our government allow its enemies this powerful advantage? The very stomach of this rebellion is the Negro in the condition of a slave. Arrest that hoe in the hands of the Negro and you smite the rebellion in the very seat of its life. To fight against

LEFT: The Emancipation Proclamation.

ABOVE: General Butler's Headquarters.

BELOW: Frederick Douglass.

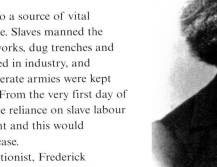

emancipation, but for the time being at least, he held back, waiting for the right moment. Regardless of Lincoln's own views on slavery, and the pressures exerted on him by the abolitionists, there were very practical reasons to abolish slavery. As the South itself admitted, its economy and culture were wedded to slavery. There were 3.5 million slaves in the 11 Confederate states and without them the Confederacy would have collapsed in a matter of months. Not only did the slaves produce the food and cash crops, they were also a source of vital manpower elsewhere. Slaves manned the transportation networks, dug trenches and fortifications, worked in industry, and ensured the Confederate armies were kept regularly supplied. From the very first day of the Confederacy, the reliance on slave labour had been paramount and this would continue to be the case.

The black abolitionist, Frederick Douglass, also noted the reliance of the South on its slave labour, and saw it as the

EMANCIPATION

ABOVE: Antietam Bridge (Burnside's Bridge).

RIGHT: Destroyed bridge at Harper's Ferry.

slaveholders, without fighting against slavery, is but a half-hearted business, and paralyses the hands engaged in it.'

As Union armies plunged into the South, pro-slavery Union officers returned slaves to their owners, under the terms of the Fugitive Slave Act, while other officers, who were against slavery, looked for ways to save them. In May 1861 General Benjamin Butler of the Union army came up with a novel solution: fugitive slaves, in his view, should be classed as contraband of war. In other words, because they contributed to the economy of the South they should be confiscated. This was ratified as policy in August 1861 with the passing of the Confiscation Act. Henceforth, all property, slaves included, would be seized by the North if they were considered to have made a direct contribution to the continuance of the rebellion against the Union.

But emancipation was slowly moving

forward. In 1862 the Union forbade officers to return slaves to their owners, and slavery was abolished in the District of Columbia and in all Union territories, while another Confiscation Act in July freed all slaves belonging to those in rebellion against the United States. The final step for Lincoln relied on there being a crushing Union victory on the battlefield, and to this end he would have to prove beyond all doubt that the tide of the war was moving in the Union's direction. His opportunity came at a

ABOVE LEFT: Confederate soldiers lying dead near Burnside's Bridge during the Battle of Antietam.

ABOVE: A cavalry orderly at Antietam.

LEFT: The battlefield of Antietam on the actual day of the battle.

THE CIVIL WAR

Battle of Fredericksburg, 13 December 1862
Thure de Thulstrup (1848–1930).
Lithograph.
Private Collection.

THE CIVIL WAR

little-known location called Antietam on 17 September 1862, when the Union army of 90,000 men clashed with almost 60,000 Confederates. The battle ended in a painful, bloody stalemate, but the Union army held and inflicted heavy losses on the Confederates. Although not an outright and striking victory, it proved for the time being that the Union army could hold the Confederates.

Lincoln issued the preliminary Emancipation Proclamation on 22 September 1862, which did not free a single individual. Moreover, the final proclamation, made on 1 January 1863, that stipulated that all slaves in states in rebellion against the Union would be 'forever free', was, in reality, still without substance. The task of freeing the slaves, apart from those who had already fled to the North, would be down to the Union army. From now on, the sight of soldiers in blue, marching through Southern towns and villages, could only mean one thing to the black population – liberation.

There were still those who thought it advisable for freed blacks to leave the United States, and there had been a botched attempt at colonization in August 1862. Lincoln asked for $60,000 to fund a project for 450 freed slaves to be settled in Haiti, but what with financial scandals, smallpox and starvation, the project failed. Black and white would somehow have to learn to live together as free men.

The approximate wartime population of blacks in the Northern states was 225,000, of which all were freed men, women and children. There were another 500,000 in the four border slave states, and upwards of another half a million who had fled from the South to cross into Union-held territory. This last group had had a mixed reception, but food was provided and schools were established with the help of abolitionists. Most significant was the desire of the men to join the Union forces, so that they could fight for the freedom they had so recently won.

At least 200,000 black men served in the Union army and navy, some three-quarters of this total being ex-slaves, the balance being freed black men from the Northern states.

Lincoln was reticent on the subject of raising black regiments. In fact he refused to allow Indiana to raise two black regiments for fear of alienating the border states. As one Washington official tactlessly remarked: 'Negroes – plantation Negroes, at least – will never make soldiers in one generation. Five white men could put a regiment to flight.' Lincoln himself had remarked in September 1862: 'If we were to arm these I fear that in a few weeks the arms would be in the hands of the rebels.'

Lincoln, Washington officials and other Northern doubters need not have concerned themselves, however. Black soldiers, almost to a man, were not only more willing to drill and learn to be soldiers, they were also more willing to stand and fight. For them, concepts such as the Union and its preservation were irrelevant. This was a war of liberation and the Confederacy had to be swept aside in order to achieve that goal.

As it turned out, pro-abolitionist officers

OPPOSITE: *Antietam National Battlefield Memorial, Sharpsburg, Maryland.*

BELOW: Camp of the Tennessee Colored Battery, Johnsonville, Tennessee.

ABOVE: Company E, 4th U.S. Colored Infantry at Fort Lincoln, Washington, D.C.

RIGHT: Picket station of colored troops stationed near Dutch Gap, Virginia, 1864.

had already been recruiting, one of the recruits being a Massachusetts man, Thomas Wentworth Higginson. This meant that the first regiments were ready by August 1863, when some 14 were created. Prior to this the 1st South Carolina Volunteers, a prototype black regiment, had already acquitted itself well in South Carolina and Georgia.

Meanwhile, a pair of black Louisiana regiments had been blooded against Confederate positions at Port Hudson, Louisiana, on the Mississippi river, as early as May 1863, leading a white officer of one of the regiments to comment: 'You have no idea how my prejudices with regard to Negro troops have been dispelled by the battle the other day.'

A fortnight later, an untried black regiment held off a concerted Confederate attack at Milliken's Bend on the Mississippi river. The Union's Assistant Secretary of State watched the action: 'The bravery of the blacks completely revolutionized the sentiment of the army with regard to the employment of Negro troops. I heard prominent officers, who formerly in private had sneered at the idea of Negroes fighting, express themselves after that as heartily in favour of it.'

On 16 July 1863 it was the turn of the

54th Massachusetts, led by its young colonel, Robert Gould Shaw. The 54th had been the first black regiment to be raised in the North. Eager to prove his men's worth, Shaw and his regiment volunteered to lead the attack on Fort Wagner, defending the approach to Charleston. Shaw was killed and his regiment suffered heavy losses, but even the Confederates could not deny their bravery. The *New York Tribune* stated after the blood repulse: 'It made Fort Wagner such a name to the coloured race as Bunker Hill has been for ninety years to the white Yankees.' (In fact black soldiers had fought at Bunker Hill, though at the time their presence was not known.)

By August 1863 both Lincoln and the pre-eminent Union commander, General Grant (the future president), were convinced that black troops were an integral part of the solution, capable of delivering a mortal blow to the South, both literally and in a wider sense. He told those who still opposed emancipation: 'You say you will not fight to free Negroes. Some of them seem willing to fight for you. There will be some black men

who can remember that, with silent tongue, and clenched teeth, and steady eye, and well poised bayonet, they have helped mankind on this great consummation; while I fear, there will be some white ones, unable to forget, with malign heart, and deceitful speech, they have strove to hinder it.'

As the Union infiltrated the Southern territories, more blacks presented themselves as recruits to the Union army. By October 1864 there were no fewer than 140 black infantry regiments, and significantly, some 38 of these took part in the invasion of Virginia in 1864, and were the first to march into Charleston and Richmond. By the time the war ended, upward of nine per cent of the total enrolment in the Union army had been black men, who would fight in nearly 40 large pitched battles and over 400 smaller engagements during the war. Around 37,000 lost their lives, many more to disease than to Confederate bullets, cannonballs or bayonets.

The Confederacy, naturally enough, reacted very badly to the recruitment and deployment of black troops, decreeing that

THE CIVIL WAR

their own slavery has never quite been explained. For many, for good or ill, they saw Southern society as their own society and acted to defend it as any other freed man would do.

Why then, with white men serving in the Confederate army and a far looser control over the millions of slaves, did the slave population of the North not rise up in rebellion? Many explanations have been put forward: some touch on the faithfulness of slaves to their masters, others to the strong powers of local militia, or home guards, operating in the countryside to control the slave population. More feasible, however, is the fact that the bulk of the slaves simply did not know what was happening. They were totally unaware not only of the Emancipation Proclamation, but also of the progress of the Union army; this was because a great many lived on plantations or in isolated rural communities where news rarely penetrated.

When Union troops were close at hand, however, they would have seen the home guards flee and their masters burying their valuables in the fields before running away. Then, with the certain knowledge of liberation, they would have headed for the blue-coated soldiers and gained their freedom.

The American Civil War is often referred to as the second American Revolution, in that it swept aside slavery and created four million more citizens of the United States. Had it not been for the thousands of courageous black soldiers in the Union army, and their stalwart determination to win and be counted as men, the Union may never have developed as it did after the Civil War.

The freedom and the civil rights that black soldiers and their white compatriots had won for themselves was eventually to be enshrined in the United States Constitution. Even though the African-American population did not achieve full civil rights until 90 years later, in the 1950s, the contribution they made towards the preservation of the Union can never be underestimated.

all white officers who led them would be charged with inciting a slave insurrection and be summarily executed. Black soldiers would likewise be hanged if it could be proven they had killed or wounded a Confederate soldier, while the rest would be returned to slavery. Although actions such as these were not carried through, captured black soldiers could expect a particularly rough time. The key restraining factor, however, was Lincoln's clear statement that if black soldiers or their white officers were executed, he would order the systematic execution of Confederate prisoners.

There were, of course, loose cannons among the Confederate ranks who would simply not accept that black soldiers and their white officers deserved the same treatment as ordinary soldiers. The most

extreme of these was Nathan Bedford Forrest, later a leading figure in the Ku Klux Klan. He was a leader of Confederate cavalry during the Civil War, often operating deep behind Union lines, and more often than not was more interested in murder, plunder and rape than military objectives. His men perpetrated what became known as the Fort Pillow Massacre on 12 April 1864 when, having overrun a Union garrison, he ordered the execution of a large number of captured black infantry.

Nonetheless, the South had begun to realize that black men did indeed make good soldiers. Black soldiers had served for the entirety of the war in Confederate white regiments, primarily as substitutes or armed servants of officers. The vexed question as to why these black men had served to prolong

CHAPTER EIGHT

EUROPE & THE WAR

FAR RIGHT: Abraham Lincoln.

BELOW RIGHT: William H. Seward.

The dominant power in the world at the time of the American Civil War was the British Empire. Both the Union and the Confederate States of America knew that whatever Britain did, the rest of the world would follow. Despite Britain's power, and its own decision to abolish slavery 30 or so years earlier, it was not about to be coerced into taking sides in the American Civil War.

The North was more outspoken when it came to outside intervention, the U.S. Secretary of State, William Seward, intimating, by way of veiled threats, what would happen if Britain or another European power gave the South its support. Seward was rabidly anti-British, and the British, in turn, considered him unscrupulous, immoral and unreliable,

treating his remarks as little more than hot air. Lincoln, on the other hand, had a far more pragmatic approach, in that he believed Britain to have no desire to be the ally of either side.

Seward had had the temerity to order European statesmen not to receive Confederate Commissioners. Fortunately for the North, Seward's lack of experience and finesse had been tempered by the presence of Charles Adams, the son of John Quincy Adams, who was the Union's minister in London. Adams was able to diffuse many difficult situations, but the North would not allow the Europeans to openly support the Confederacy, knowing that the Europeans secretly favoured the South.

Support for the Confederacy in Britain came from many factions, from Quakers to Roman Catholics, and all believed the North was suppressing the South. In political circles, the Tories backed the South and found staunch allies among the radicals and the liberals, while in society at large, titled members of the House of Lords through to the leaders of the working classes all favoured the Confederate cause. The underlying problem had been a statement in which Lincoln had clearly indicated that the Civil War was not against slavery, but a war to preserve the Union, making it more natural that those fighting for their independence should be supported.

The Confederates earnestly believed that Britain, whose industrial heart was the cotton industry, would have to break the Union blockade or face economic disaster. Southern cotton was essential to Britain, and by the winter of 1862/63 the shortages had begun to bite and over 200,000 British workers were without work. Around half a

million people were directly affected by the Union blockade that prevented cotton from reaching Britain.

France was no less affected, in that it obtained 90 per cent of its raw cotton imports from the Southern states. It also had pro-Confederate sympathizers who were in favour of giving direct military aid to the Confederacy. But the French emperor, Napoleon III, was terrified at the prospect of siding with the Confederate States of America, especially if Britain remained neutral.

Britain ultimately found other sources of raw cotton, so the shortage was short-lived.

THE CIVIL WAR

In the meantime there was money to be made from manufacturing weapons and ships. The sad fact is that the South did not really have a foreign policy and it was never able to clear the first hurdle – that of being recognized as independent from the Union. This would prove disastrous and allow the Europeans to sit out the war, removing the risk to them of choosing the wrong side as their ally.

The spring of 1861 had seen some hope for the South. Both Britain and France had recognized the Union as a 'belligerent'. This was an important step and inferred that they did not accept that the Union was engaged in an internal fight, but was acting against another country. These were the first signs that Europe was coming round to the idea of the South as an entity separate from the United States. Seward was enraged and it seemed that, for a while, his ravings would tip the balance and Britain would indeed side with the South. All the signs were there that Britain would first recognize the Confederacy and then offer it actual assistance in resisting the North.

The flames of war were fanned in November 1861 when two Confederate commissioners, James Murray Mason and

John Slidell, headed for Britain, hoping to secure recognition for the Confederate States of America. They boarded the British ship *Trent*, but the following day, in contravention of international law, Captain Charles Wilkes of the U.S. vessel *San Jacinto* boarded the *Trent* and ordered it to be searched, when he seized the two men. The British demanded an apology for the outrage and the immediate release of Mason and Slidell; even Seward recognized it had been a step too far, and Lincoln concurred; consequently, the North had no choice but to capitulate or face certain and drastic repercussions from the British.

Wilkes was hung out to dry, forced to take the blame for the incident. The two men were released, but this had been the closest the British would ever come to throwing their weight behind the Confederacy.

There was still a hope of this happening following the Second Battle of Bull Run (Manassas) in August 1862, but Britain saw the turning of the tide and decided to remain neutral.

In 1864 Napoleon III of France threw his hat into the ring in the desperate hope of reliving the successes of his uncle,

Napoleon Bonaparte. Archduke Maximilian of Austria, having been approached by Mexican monarchists, allowed himself to be persuaded by Napoleon III into becoming Emperor of Mexico.

Theoretically, Napoleon III had acted at the right moment: the American Civil War precluded military intervention by the Union and the South had offered him support in return for recognition. The plan was short-lived, however; before long, there was a popular uprising in Mexico, led by Benito Juárez, and the Emperor Maximilian was executed.

As the Union began to amass victories towards the end of the Civil War, so it had become more vociferous in its protests against French involvement in Mexico. On the one hand the Union feared the French would militarily support the South, but it could not intervene itself. In the end French troops withdrew from Mexico and left Maximilian to his fate.

In the end, the South's attempts to gain recognition and help from Europe came to nought. Great Britain remained neutral, as did France and Prussia, and even the

FAR LEFT: James Murray Mason.

LEFT: John Slidell.

BELOW: Soldiers lying dead during the Battle of Gettysburg.

EUROPE & THE WAR

ABOVE: Lt. Col. James J. Smith and officers of the 69th New York Infantry (Irish Brigade).

BELOW: The Alabama *with the* Brilliante *in the background.*

Spanish, with hopes of holding onto their Caribbean possessions, kept out of the conflict. Sweden, Belgium and the Vatican also failed to act, having waited in vain for leadership to come from Great Britain.

The Russian Tsar, Alexander II, had even refused to see the Confederate envoys. Russia had little need of American manufactured goods or food and in fact saw a strong, united America as a useful force with which to constrain Britain.

What concerned Britain and France most were the possible losses inflicted on them by the Union blockade, though in reality their vessels were constantly breaking them. The French wanted harbours to be free of blockade, but the North would not agree. As a consequence, many British and French vessels worked as privateers, which was an effective way of getting goods in and out of the South.

Confederate ships were built in both British and French ports, Liverpool being a prime example; it provided at least 70 blockade-runners to the South between 1862 and 1865, some of which were crewed by British sailors, while others were sold direct to the Confederacy. The *Alabama*, *Florida* and *Shenandoah*, warships that preyed on Northern shipping, were also supplied by Britain to the Confederacy, as were ironclad rams, though these were bought outright by the Royal Navy as a safeguard against Union protests.

Neither the Union nor the Confederacy could have hoped to have waged war without the masses of muskets built in Britain and shipped across the Atlantic in vast numbers. The Enfield model, used by both sides in huge quantities, was either

manufactured in Britain or made under licence in the United States.

Another considerable contribution to the American Civil War was the enormous flow of immigrants, who continued to arrive despite the conflict. Between 1861 and 1863 alone, 180,000 Irish arrived in the United States, while a conservative estimate of 100,000 enrolled in the Union army. In fact, virtually all Irish regiments flourished, including the famous Irish Brigade of the Union army.

In fact, men from all over Europe could be found in the ranks of the Confederate armies, some, of course, being adventurers, while others were fighting for their own perceptions of liberty and independence.

In the end it was not the bluster and threats of the North that ensured Europe's neutrality. Britain, in particular, had taken a cautious and pragmatic view, having various interests in other parts of the world that required its attention. But this tended to work in the Union's favour; even though the Union had failed to win European support, by working to ensure that Europe did not support the South, the Union had gained more freedom to deal with the rebellion in its own way.

THE CIVIL WAR

CHAPTER NINE

THE ROAD TO VICTORY

RIGHT: Men repairing a single-track railroad after the Battle of Stone's River, Murfreesboro, 31 December 1862–2 January 1863.

BELOW: General Buell.

With all the activity, manoeuvring and fighting taking place in the East, it is easy to forget that there was also a war going on in the West. On 9 June 1862 Union General Buell took control of the Army of the Ohio, aiming to tackle Confederate troops in East Tennessee. The first target was to be Chattanooga, though there was a problem in that the Confederate cavalry, under the command of Forrest and Morgan, was continually raiding the area through which he needed to pass. These raiders regularly attacked Union outposts, bridges and supply columns.

On 30 August 1862 Union troops advanced against Richmond, Kentucky.

Many of the Northern soldiers were raw recruits and it was an unmitigated disaster, with nearly 1,000 killed or wounded and over 4,500 captured.

Focus then switched to the Cumberland Gap, which was something of a gateway into East Tennessee. Union troops were stationed there by the end of August, in the hope that

proclamation to Kentucky, asking it to support the Confederacy, and a provisional governor was inaugurated on 4 October.

After the Confederate army, under Van Dorn, had been defeated at Corinth, Mississippi, on 4 October, Bragg found himself pretty much on his own. Bragg's main army was at Louisville and Buell made several diversionary attacks, which culminated in an inconclusive engagement at Perryville on 8 October. After this, Bragg's army moved to Murfreesboro, Tennessee, in what was effectively a retreat, destroying any supplies that could not be carried. Buell gave chase and the cavalry clashed 26 times along the route.

Buell's reluctance to close with the Confederates again angered Washington and he was relieved of his command. William Rosecrans, who assumed command of the Army of the Cumberland, as the force was now known, replaced him on 20 October.

On 26 December Rosecrans finally ordered the army to march on Murfreesboro, but it was continually harassed by Confederate cavalry as it advanced. The first main engagement took place on 30 December 1862, but both sides were content to fire artillery at one another.

LEFT: **Battle of Lookout Mountain, 24 November 1863, Army of the Cumberland**
Lithograph by Kurz & Allison, c.1889.

BELOW FAR LEFT: General George W. Morgan.

BELOW CENTRE LEFT: General James Longstreet.

BELOW LEFT: General Edmund Kirby-Smith.

Morgan's supplies would be cut off. The Confederate troops tried to dislodge them and a concerted effort was made on 17 September. This time the Union troops withdrew and on 3 October reached the Ohio river.

While the Confederates were threatening the Cumberland Gap, Confederate Generals Bragg and Kirby-Smith decided to launch a campaign against Buell, who had concentrated his troops at Nashville. When he heard the Confederates were heading in his direction, he left a holding force at Nashville and took the bulk of his army to Bowling Green. After achieving a victory at Munfordville, the Confederates issued a

W. T. Trego. 1895.

THE CIVIL WAR

The Cavalry
W.T. Trego, 19th century.
Lithograph.
Private Collection.

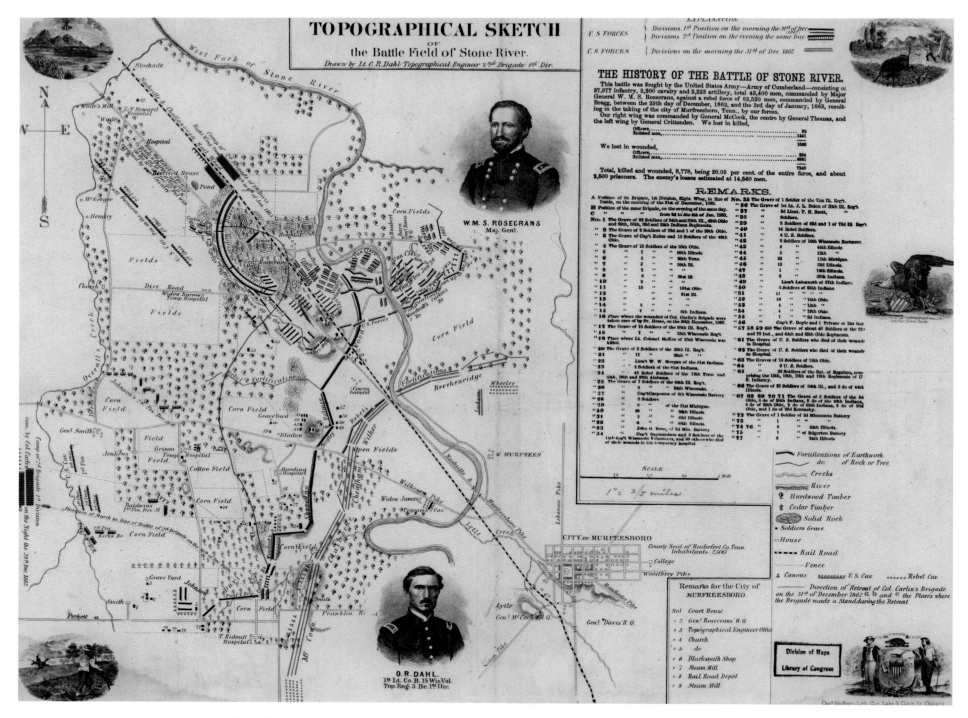

Topographical Sketch of the Battlefield of Stone [Stones] River
Drawn by Lt. O.R. Dahl, 2nd Brigade, 1st Division, 1862.

The following day, the two armies were quiet and the Confederates believed that Rosecrans was about to retreat. To their horror, however, the Confederates discovered that the Union force had taken the opportunity to dig in, and the Confederates were forced to drive the Union troops out of their entrenchments. But the assault was disastrous and cost the Confederate army over 10,000 casualties out of its total force of 40,000. Bragg retreated and Rosecrans entered Murfreesboro.

Bragg's army had simply not been strong enough to deal with Rosecrans' force, which in this campaign had amounted to some 43,000. After some wrangling, General Longstreet's corps of the Army of Northern Virginia was sent to reinforce Bragg, but failed to reach him before another major battle took place. Bragg had established his base at Chattanooga by July 1863, but by

early September he realized how dangerous his position was, with a Union army of some 57,000 bearing down on him.

On the morning of 19 September, Union troops were approaching Chickamauga. There was a skirmish between dismounted cavalry to begin with, but both sides began to reinforce. When the general engagement took place the following day, 20 September, the Confederates took the offensive. The Union left was thrown into confusion and reinforcements did not reach the front in time. By this stage Longstreet's troops had arrived and he was thrown into the battle, hitting the Union right. The Union troops held and both sides were badly mauled. With great reluctance Rosecrans ordered his army to withdraw from what had been a bloody engagement. Rosecrans had deployed 58,000 men and had suffered over 16,000 casualties, while the Confederates, including

ABOVE LEFT: General Braxton Bragg.

ABOVE: General William S. Rosecrans, Army of the Ohio.

General Grant Looking over the Battlefield at Fort Donelson, c.1863
Paul Phillipoteaux (1846–1923).
Oil on canvas.
Chicago Historical Museum, Chicago.

ABOVE: **The Battle of Lookout Mountain (Battle above Clouds)** *James Walker, 1874.*

OPPOSITE: *Sketch of the Battles of Chattanooga, 23–26 November 1863.*

Longstreet, had some 66,000 men engaged and had lost nearly 18,500.

It now seemed that the Confederacy was about to sweep the Union forces out of Tennessee, and desperate action was needed. Troops were detached from the Army of the Potomac, but it was necessary for them to travel on over 1,100 miles (1770km) of connecting railroad lines. Some of the units got there by 30 September, but others did not arrive until 16 October, the day on which Grant was given command of the Military Division of the Mississippi. This would

incorporate the departments of the Ohio, the Cumberland, the Tennessee and responsibilities in Mississippi.

One of Grant's first actions was to ensure his supply lines were properly protected. Having established his main base at Chattanooga, on a bend of the Tennessee river, he could now be assured that by using the river as the main supply line, his troops would be adequately fed and equipped.

The Confederates, meanwhile, keeping a close eye on the Union force, had established positions on high ground around

Chattanooga. Their positions ran from the East Tennessee & Georgia Railroad in the north, along Missionary Ridge to Rossville, and additional forces were posted on Lookout Mountain to the south-west of Chattanooga. With more troops still arriving, Grant determined to dislodge the Confederate army.

At 1540 on 24 November signal guns were fired and nearly 25,000 Union troops rushed forward to storm Confederate positions along Missionary Ridge. The assault was so overwhelming that the

ABOVE: Blockhouse on the Nashville & Chattanooga Railroad during the Battle of Chattanooga.

ABOVE RIGHT: Confederate prisoners, Chattanooga.

RIGHT: Chattanooga from the north.

THE CIVIL WAR

Umbrella Rock on Lookout Mountain, Chattanooga, Tennessee.

ABOVE: Scouts and guides of the Army of the Potomac at Brandy Station, Virginia, March 1864.

RIGHT: **Battle of Missionary Ridge, 25 November 1863**
Chromolithograph, Cosack & Co., c.1886.

FAR RIGHT: The Chickamauga Battlefield, drawn by J.C. McElroy, c.1895.

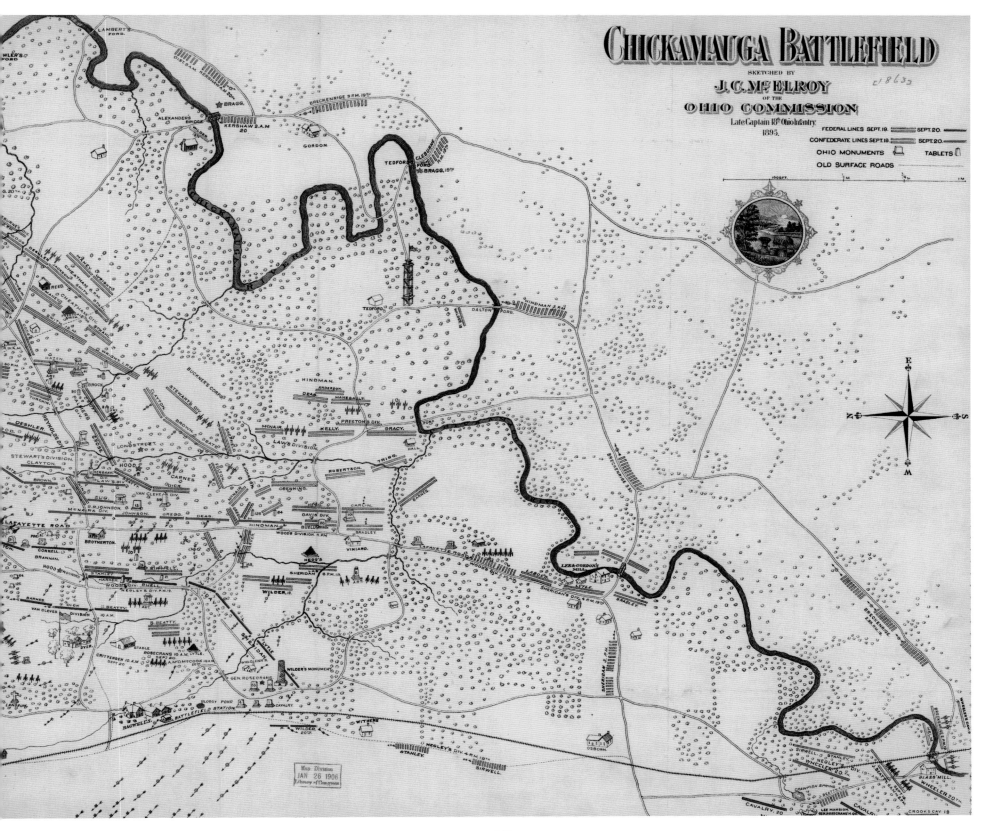

THE ROAD TO VICTORY

RIGHT: U.S. Military Telegraph battery wagon, Army of the Potomac, Petersburg, Virginia, 1864.

BELOW: Lt. General Leonidas Polk, officer of the Confederate army.

Confederates, after firing a few shots, fell back in disorder. Bragg ordered his troops to fall back to Chickamauga.

Grant had discovered on 4 November that Longstreet had moved towards Knoxville to threaten General Burnside's Union army. In order to force Longstreet to return to the front near Chattanooga, Grant determined to launch an assault. Burnside's forces were well dug in and it would not be an easy task to dislodge him. The assaults against Burnside were timed for 28 November, but bad weather put the engagement back a day. No sooner had Longstreet's men been committed, than a telegram arrived telling him to return immediately to support Bragg, with the result that the siege against Burnside was broken almost as soon as it had begun.

Soon after, Longstreet rejoined the Army of Northern Virginia. General Polk replaced Bragg, but on 27 December Polk, in turn, was replaced by General Joseph E.

Johnston. Things were not going all that well for the Union army during the winter of 1863/64. Sherman, in command of the Department of the Tennessee, was still suffering attacks from roving bands of Confederate raiders, and decided to raise a large cavalry force and attack Meridian. The attack got under way on 3 February 1864, with the cavalry covering 150 miles (240km) in 11 days. Everything that Sherman's cavalry could not take with them they destroyed, including railroads.

On 2 March 1864 General Grant was given overall command of the Union armies, in the hope that he would co-ordinate the Union effort. After reorganizing the Union armies, Grant began to frame the strategy by which the Confederacy would be defeated. Sherman's force amounted to nearly 99,000 men and he would attack Johnston. Thomas had over 60,000 men in Chattanooga, McPherson had 25,000 in Huntsville,

THE CIVIL WAR

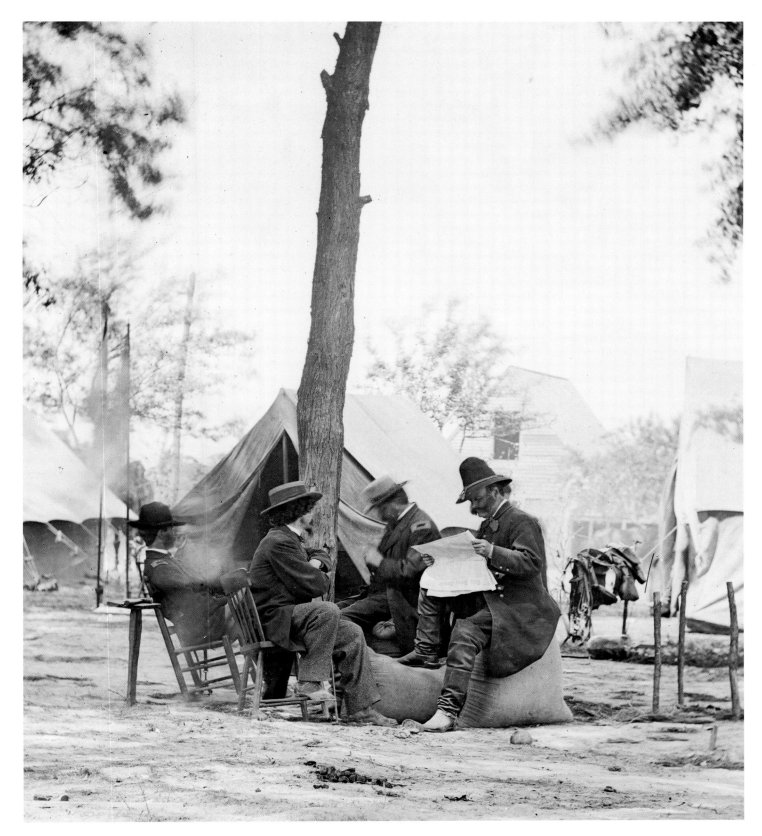

General Burnside (reading newpaper) with Mathew B. Brady (nearest tree) at the Army of the Potomac headquarters (possibly at Cold Harbor, Virginia).

THE ROAD TO VICTORY

RIGHT: Kennesaw Mountain.

BELOW: Pine Mountain.

OPPOSITE LEFT: General George
H. Thomas.

OPPOSITE LEFT BELOW:
Spotsylvania Courthouse.

OPPOSITE RIGHT: General
Ambrose Burnside.

Alabama, and Schofield had 13,500 in Knoxville, Tennessee. Facing them were just 50,000 Confederates under Johnston. Sherman launched his Georgia campaign on 5 May 1864. There was heavy fighting and very soon the Confederates were in full retreat.

Johnston eventually fell back to New Hope, where he amassed 64,000 men. The Confederates were occupying three prominent hills: Kennesaw, Pine Mountain and Lost Mountain. Sherman's armies moved up to engage. After dreadful weather it was finally decided that the Union troops would assault the Confederate line on 27 June 1864, with attacks coming in along the entire 10-mile (16-km) front. This had mixed results and in some places ground was taken, but losses were high. When the Union army threatened his flank a few days later, Johnston withdrew from Kennesaw.

Sherman ordered his cavalry to strike

Sketch showing positions and entrenchments of the Army of North Virginia during the battles for Spotsylvania Courthouse from 9–21 May 1864.

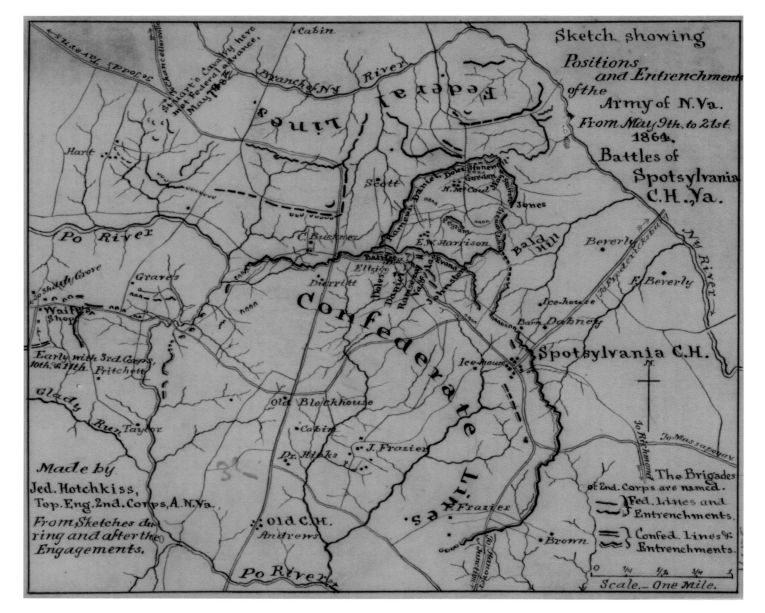

deep behind Confederate lines and into Alabama, before beginning his advance towards Atlanta. Johnston was unsure what to do, and General Hood replaced him on 17 July. Hood had acquired an army in fairly poor condition and it had lost nearly a third of its strength, there being a mere 49,000 men when Hood became commander. Hood was determined to defend Atlanta and saw his opportunity on 20 July, as Union troops pushed forward. They clashed at Peachtree Creek, but the Confederates were no match for the strong Union force. Hood pulled out

of contact and the Union army moved on, ever closer to Atlanta.

Despite bitter counter-offensives, Sherman's army was just 20 miles (32km) south of Atlanta by 2 September 1864. Hood had decided to abandon the city for fear of being surrounded. He decided to attempt to draw Sherman back towards the mountains and there, in restricted ground, to defeat him.

By 1 October Hood was heading for Nashville, by which stage he had around 40,000 men and was being pursued by

60,000 under Sherman. It was then learned that Hood had surrounded the Federal supply base at Allatoona, held by fewer than 900 men. The attack failed and Hood broke off, believing that a large Union force was close by.

Sherman now decided to force Hood to face him. He would march across Georgia and head for Savannah and Charleston and Hood would have to follow. By 31 October Hood had reached Tuscumbia, Alabama, but it had been left to General Thomas to deal with Hood, because by 10 November

ABOVE LEFT: General Cadmus Wilcox of the Confederate army.

ABOVE: Maj. General George G. Meade, officer of the Federal army, with corps commanders, June 1865.

LEFT: City Point, Virginia.

Sherman was on his way to bring devastation to the heart of the Confederacy.

Meanwhile, in the East, the Army of the Potomac had reorganized, having been strengthened over the winter of 1863/64. On 4 May 1864, under the direct command of Grant and ably assisted by Meade, it was determined to launch a major offensive. Throughout the winter, Lee had been settled around the Fredericksburg and

Chancellorsville area. He could call on some 62,000 men, whereas Grant and Meade had 118,000 at their disposal.

Lead elements of the Union army attacked Confederate outposts close to the Rapidan river on 4 May. The main army crossed the following day and headquarters were set up at the Wilderness Tavern. Lee could not afford to engage until Longstreet's force rejoined him on 6 May, but Grant was

THE CIVIL WAR

OPPOSITE LEFT: *General Matthew Butler, Confederate army.*

OPPOSITE RIGHT: *General Sheridan (right), General Katz (seated) and a friend.*

LEFT: *Allatoona Pass, Georgia, looking north.*

LEFT BELOW: *Allatoona Pass, looking south.*

OPPOSITE LEFT: *Outside the former residence of General John Bell Hood, near Atlanta.*

OPPOSITE RIGHT: *Dead Confederate soldiers after Ewell's attack at Spotsylvania.*

LEFT: *A soldier's burial, the scene of Ewell's attack at Mrs Allsop's house, near Spotsylvania Courthouse.*

**Battle of the Wilderness, Attack at
Spotsylvania Courthouse, Virginia,
1864**

Alonzo Chappel (1828–87).
Oil on canvas
Chicago Historical Museum, Chicago.

THE CIVIL WAR

OPPOSITE: Port Royal on the Rappahannock river, during Grant's Wilderness Campaign.

LEFT: Drewry's Bluff, on the James river, where the battle took place in May 1862.

PIERRE GUSTAVE TOUTANT BEAUREGARD (1818–93)

Born in Louisiana, Beauregard attended West Point in 1838, graduating second in his class and acquiring the nickname 'The Little Napoleon'. By 1861 he had been made superintendent at West

Point, but resigned his commission to become a brigadier general in the Confederate army, and it was Beauregard's troops who attacked and took Fort Sumter. He took tactical command at the First Bull Run, and is credited with drafting the attack orders for the Battle of Shiloh. After he was forced to evacuate his supply base in Mississippi, he was relieved of his command in June 1862, returning to lead the Confederates in the Carolinas. Beauregard's greatest victory was at Drury's Bluff against Benjamin Butler. He managed to ward off Union attempts to take Petersburg while Robert E. Lee was positioned north of the James river. In September 1864 Beauregard returned to the Western theatre and operated with Hood and Taylor, but they were unsuccessful in preventing Sherman from marching to the sea. When the war ended, Beauregard refused offers of a command abroad. He was involved in railroads and became Louisiana's Adjutant General. He died on 20 February 1893 and was buried at Metairie, Louisiana.

already pushing cavalry forward and it now seemed certain there would be a battle. Grant was aware that Longstreet was due to arrive with 12,000 reinforcements.

On 6 May, at 0500, the Union army attacked in force, the blow falling on Major General Wilcox's division. The Confederates began to fall back, with Lee desperately hoping that Longstreet would arrive. Eventually Longstreet did arrive, halted the Confederate retreat and began to push the Union army back. Unfortunately, Longstreet was hit by a bullet, causing severe bleeding. That night the pinewoods of the Wilderness caught fire due to the shelling and many men were burned to death.

On the morning of 7 May Grant planned to head south-east towards Spotsylvania Courthouse. Grant had seen the danger as a smaller Union force, under Butler, had landed at City Point on 5 May, and that Lee could swiftly move towards Richmond and destroy Butler's force. Lee had ordered elements of his army to head for

Spotsylvania, but this was delayed due to the forest fires and the fact that Union cavalry was engaged at Todd's Tavern, close by.

Sheridan, at the head of the Union cavalry, planned a raid on Richmond, beginning on 9 May 1864, and he would be absent for 16 days. Confederate trains were intercepted and Union prisoners freed, and warehouses containing rations for the army were destroyed. Eventually J.E.B. Stuart's cavalry caught up with Sheridan and there were running skirmishes from 10 May. Stuart's cavalry reached Yellow Tavern before Sheridan, taking up defensive positions around the Telegraph Road, and at around 1600 on 11 May Sheridan's cavalry arrived. It managed to drive back Stuart's left; Stuart rushed to rally his men and in the confusing fight an unhorsed Union trooper saw a mounted Confederate officer to his side. He fired his pistol, hitting Stuart, who died the following day. He had graduated from West Point in 1854 and was only 31 years old.

OPPOSITE BELOW LEFT: The 12th Pennsylvania Volunteers at Bloody Angle.

OPPOSITE BELOW RIGHT: A party of the 50th New York Engineers engaged in road-building along the banks of the North Anna River.

LEFT: Drewry's Bluff, interior of the Confederate Fort Darling.

Meanwhile the Confederates had taken up positions on high ground around Spotsylvania, arranging themselves in a semi-circle, with Spotsylvania Courthouse within the 3-mile (5-km) defensive line. Lee's troops had been digging in from the evening of 8 May, felling trees and piling up earthworks; part of the defensive works would become known as Bloody Angle. This was a salient point in the Confederate line held by men from Ewell's corps. The fighting was so frenzied in that area that the ground was soon covered with layer upon layer of bodies. Grant fanatically pushed his men forward, regardless of casualties, and at around midnight on 12 May the Confederate army withdrew. Grant had lost nearly 13,500 men and the Confederates around 10,000.

There were five days of continual rain after Spotsylvania, and the news for the Union was not good. Union troops had been defeated at Newmarket, at Drewry's Bluff, and in Louisiana. On 19 May Grant decided to make his new base at Port Royal, on the Rappahannock, but on the same day Lee was on the offensive, attacking 6,000 untried Union troops under General Taylor. Fortunately, the Union troops were able to hold out.

On 20 May Grant took the initiative, though he was taking a chance in splitting up his corps, and moved towards Richmond,

ABOVE: Hanover Courthouse, Virginia.

RIGHT: The Peninsula Campaign, May–August 1862: a Howitzer gun is captured by Butterfield's brigade near Hanover Courthouse.

OPPOSITE: Hanover Junction, Virginia.

ABOVE: General Fitzhugh Lee.

RIGHT: General Winfield Scott Hancock.

taking the route from Guiney's Station to Bowling Green, then Milford. The armies clashed at North Anna Bridge on the evening of 23 May and once again the Confederates were thrown back. By now Grant was certain Lee was in difficulties and told Washington: 'Lee is really whipped. The prisoners we now take show it, and the action of his army shows it unmistakeably. I may be mistaken, but I feel that our success over Lee's army is already assured.' Grant could not have been more wrong.

By the morning of 27 May Sheridan's cavalry had reached Hanover Ferry. This allowed the Union army to cross the

THE CIVIL WAR

Pamunkey the following day. Lee was determined to prevent Grant from finding an open road to Richmond. He was asking Richmond for more troops and was determined that Grant should not reach the Chickahominy river. Lee wanted General Beauregard to join him in his efforts to crush Grant, but Beauregard was of the opinion that Lee should be defending along the Chickahominy and that he should be sending troops to him.

On 15 May Lee had learned from a captured despatch that upwards of 25,000 new Union troops were en route to Grant from Washington. Beauregard and Lee met together on 29 May, the upshot being that Lee would engage Grant with whatever troops he had. On 30 May Sheridan's cavalry managed to move towards Hanover Courthouse, where Confederate cavalry was encountered. Sheridan was able to overrun the Confederate defences, losing 228 men in

the process, while the Confederates lost around 450.

At 1700 on the same day, Lieutenant General Jubal Early, who had succeeded Ewell, attacked the Union left, and additional reinforcements were required to push the Confederates off. On the same afternoon there was further cavalry action near Old Church and the Confederate cavalry was pushed back towards Cold Harbor. On 31 May Sheridan attacked

The Chickahominy river.

Confederate cavalry under General Fitzhugh Lee, close to the crossroads at Cold Harbor. The Confederates were pushed back for some distance and Sheridan held the ground.

It was now clear that Grant was advancing towards Cold Harbor. Lee immediately seized the chance to turn

Grant's flank and moved troops out of his main front line, placing them a mile to the north-west of Cold Harbor. Awaiting the Union thrust were around 15,000 Confederates. The Confederates attacked at dawn on 1 June, but met with almost immediate disaster. Lawrence Keitt, leading the attack and riding at the head of his

brigade, was shot within minutes and his regiment broke for cover.

Things were shaping up for a major confrontation. Lee expected Grant to attack in force on 2 June, but the attack had been pushed back to 0430 on 3 June. This would be the principal action in the Battle of Cold Harbor and would turn out to be the single

OPPOSITE: A cooking tent at Fredericksburg during the Wilderness Campaign.

ABOVE: Soldiers filling canteens at Fredericksburg during the Wilderness Campaign.

THE CIVIL WAR

The Battle of Fredericksburg on 13 December 1862
Frederick Cavada, 19th century.
Oil on canvas.
Atwater Kent Museum of Philadelphial
Courtesy of the Historical Society of
Pennsylvania Collection.

THE ROAD TO VICTORY

most expensive assault in terms of casualties that the Union army had ever launched. Three corps were moving forward to take part in the attack, but during the night it had rained and the ground was muddy. It was also difficult for the corps to keep in touch with one another due to the contours of the terrain. No sooner had the Union troops come into view than they were subjected to fire. In General Hancock's 2nd Corps no fewer than eight colonels died in the first assault alone, each of the corps commanders having been told to attack with their entire force. It was an unmitigated disaster and in just half an hour Grant's army suffered 7,000 casualties. By 0730 the battle was over. Reluctantly Grant called it a day at 1200.

An unfortunate incident occurred between Grant and Lee after the battle of Cold Harbor, when time was wasted while the two wrangled over a ceasefire that would allow their wounded to be gathered up. Despite men left groaning on the battlefield, neither would concede the terms of the ceasefire, and it took 48 hours for them to finally agree, by which time hundreds of men, left lying in the mud, had died from their wounds.

THE CIVIL WAR

It seems that Lee was the more pleased with the results of the battle. He wrote to the Confederate Secretary of War: 'So far every attack of the enemy has been repulsed. Repeated attacks were made. They were met with great steadiness and repulsed in every instance. The attack extended to our extreme left, under General Early, with like results. Later in the day it was twice renewed against General Heth but was repulsed with loss. Our loss today has been small, and our success, under the blessing of God, all that we could expect.' Indeed, Lee's force had probably lost 1,200 killed and wounded against at least 11,000 Union casualties.

So far the Wilderness Campaign, with its huge death toll, had been too costly. The only thing that gave comfort to the Union,

ABOVE: Lt. General Jubal Early.

RIGHT: Major General Franz Sigel.

FAR RIGHT: Major General Philip H. Sheridan.

BELOW: Point Lookout, Maryland, with views of Hammond General Hospital and prisoner-of-war depot.

THE CIVIL WAR

Gaines' Mill in ruins.

at this time, was the persistent progress of Sherman, who was steadily marching towards the sea and the Carolinas. It was difficult to maintain morale, but Grant's army, despite the losses, was still growing.

Lee feared Grant would now move against Petersburg, but in the meantime he had some breathing space and sent Jubal Early from Gaines' Mill into the Shenandoah Valley. It was a diversionary attack: he knew that Early could deal with the Union troops under General Hunter in the Shenandoah Valley and after that he would be able to cross the Potomac and threaten Washington.

Waves of panic struck the Union ranks in the belief that Early was at the head of 20,000 men (it was in fact half that number). Harper's Ferry was abandoned and 5,000 men, under General Sigel, crossed the Potomac river and occupied the Maryland Heights, joined by the troops that had evacuated Harper's Ferry.

By 6 July Early was in Sharpsburg, where an opportunity had arisen. There were 17,000 Confederate prisoners-of-war at Point Lookout at the tip of Maryland, just at the point where the Potomac flows into Chesapeake Bay. The operation to free the prisoners was being controlled by Colonel John Taylor Wood, who proposed to attack the camp using gunboats, before linking up with Early close to Baltimore. The 17,000 men could then join Early's army. The plan, however, was abandoned as the Confederates learned the Union government had been

Sheridan's Famous Ride at the Battle of Cedar Creek, Virginia, in 1864
Thure de Thulstrup (1848–1930).
Chromolithograph.
Private collection.

A Confederate Scout of General Turner Ashby at the Valley near Luray and New Hacket
J.A. Collins, 19th Century.
Chicago Historical Museum, Chicago.

THE CIVIL WAR

removing the prisoners from Point Lookout since 10 June.

Early presented a considerable problem. He was marching towards the Potomac, but the garrison defences surrounding Washington consisted of fewer than 10,000 men, while some 53 forts, over a perimeter of 37 miles (59km), surrounded the city itself. Each of the forts had a liberal allocation of artillery pieces, but they would need 25,000 infantry, 9,000 artillerymen and around 3,000 cavalry to man them all.

Grant was ordered to send men back to Washington, beginning with over 2,000 men, followed by additional divisions. Troops were rushed from Baltimore and by 7 July detachments of the Army of the Potomac, sent by Grant, had arrived in Baltimore. As Early approached the Monocacy river on Saturday 9 July 1864 he encountered Union troops waiting for him on the east bank. After a full day's fighting, the Confederates

forced the Union contingent of around 6,000 back, leaving the road to Washington open, there being no major Union formations between the Confederate army and the capital. There was understandable panic.

Early continued towards Washington, sending advance units down the Georgetown Pike, while his main force moved from Rockville towards Silver Spring. He was on the road to Seventh Street Pike, a main road leading directly into Washington. Near Silver Spring, Early was delayed by a small detachment of Union cavalry, but shortly after midday he was in sight of Fort Stevens, where he rested. He noted the defensive positions were barely manned, but suddenly there was dust on the horizon, from which a column of Union infantry emerged; Union artillery batteries began to open fire on the Confederates. Early had around 8,000 infantry and 40 artillery pieces, and if he

was to move on Washington he would have to be quick.

As the hours passed, more Union troops took up positions in the fort and the defence works around the Georgetown Pike. Early was concerned that if he gave battle now, and lost, his men would be trapped; Union forces were undoubtedly in possession of the passes around South Mountain and were covering the fords of the Upper Potomac. As the day drew on, even more Union troops began to arrive, some on steamers. Perhaps Early's chance to catch Washington unawares had been lost, but he was determined to assault the fortifications on 12 July.

The defence of Fort Stevens was witnessed by no other than President Lincoln himself. Union forces were now strong enough to deal with Early on the open field, but still Early held back, concerned that his men would be

Company K, 3rd Regiment, Massachusetts Heavy Artillery at Fort Stevens, District of Columbia.

ABOVE: Ruins of the Franklin Courthouse at Chambersburg, Pennsylvania, destroyed by Confederate forces in 1864.

ABOVE RIGHT: Chambersburg Pike.

RIGHT: General Custer and a dog, The Peninsula, Virginia.

slaughtered. Finally it was the Union forces that prompted action by opening fire with artillery at 1800. Union infantry moved forward, but met with determined resistance, and after taking nearly 300 casualties the Union troops withdrew, back to their defence works. Early knew full well that his opportunity had been lost and made plans to withdraw. He left just 200 men behind to act as a rearguard and his footsore men began to fall back through Rockville to Poolesville before crossing the Potomac river at White's Ford on 14 July. He allowed his men to rest at Leesburg, then headed into the Shenandoah Valley.

The Shenandoah Valley had been of importance during the entire war, being the place where General Stonewall Jackson made his name, having beaten and confounded far larger Union forces with a relatively small force throughout late 1861 and into 1862. The Shenandoah Valley was no less important by 1864, but this time the situation had been reversed, and

FAR LEFT: *General George Custer.*

LEFT: *Major General John McAllister Schofield.*

BELOW: *The Battle of Winchester, fought in the Shenandoah Valley.*

considerable numbers of Union troops were operating in the Shenandoah Valley. On 15 May 1864 there had been a battle at Newmarket, which the Confederates had won, but it had not stopped the Union army from destroying houses, factories and mills.

It was decided that a Confederate force would enter Pennsylvania and collect $100,000 in gold as payment for the damage

THE ROAD TO VICTORY

ABOVE: General Sherman near Atlanta, Georgia, in 1864.

RIGHT: Map of the Battle of Nashville, 15–16 December 1864.

OPPOSITE: A street in Savannah, Georgia, today.

Martinsburg on 18 September and there was another fight at Winchester the next day, the Confederates being forced back each time. By 20 September the Union army had reoccupied the defensive positions that it had held before along Cedar Creek.

The main Confederate position was on Fishers Hill, which Union troops stormed at dawn on 22 September. Having taken heavy casualties, Early's Confederates began to retire towards Charlottesville, and with the exception of Confederate raiding and some cavalry clashes, all was quiet until mid-October.

It was now 19 October and Sheridan had been to Washington. He was returning to Winchester when, at 0600, he received intelligence that there was firing in the direction of his forces. In what was later known as Sheridan's Ride, he proceeded cross-country to avoid roads and wounded men. Indeed, his army was engaged against Early's Confederates. Sheridan arrived on the battlefield at 1030, with an army that seemed on the verge of collapse, though his presence brought fresh hope. Even though

done in the Shenandoah. A Confederate force of only a brigade, under Brigadier General McCausland, crossed the River Potomac on 29 July. He made for Chambersburg and when the Union inhabitants refused to pay he burned the place to the ground. On his return to Virginia, McCausland was intercepted at Moorfield, West Virginia, on 7 August, losing 500 men at a minimal cost to the Union force.

On 11 August Union cavalry, under General George Custer, attacked Early's troops 3 miles (5km) from Winchester, forcing them back, and there was another sharp fight close to Strasburg the following day. Confederate cavalry raided Union supply trains on 13 August and due to this and many other problems the Union troops fell back to Charlestown.

The Union army, now under the command of Major General Sheridan, went back on the offensive in early September, reaching Berryville on 3 September, where it dug in. The Confederates were driven out of

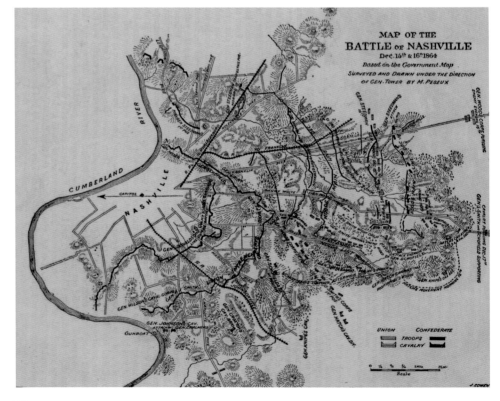

the Union camp had been overrun by Confederates, who had grabbed equipment and food, which they had not seen for some months, Sheridan organized attacks and eventually his infantry began to advance once again. Early pulled away but many of his men were caught, overburdened with loot, though he eventually established a new line 7 miles (11km) below Mount Jackson. There were several other small battles, but this was the last major engagement in the 1864 Shenandoah Valley Campaign.

During the campaign Union casualties had been close on 17,000, while Confederate casualties are difficult to assess, but at Cedar Creek alone the Confederates lost close on 3,000 men.

The struggle for Tennessee was about to intensify. Sherman had already left the area and was marching through Georgia. This left almost 60,000 Union troops, under Major General Thomas, in Tennessee, while General Hood, who determined to launch a new campaign in Tennessee and destroy Thomas's army, commanded the Confederates. The campaign got under way

OPPOSITE: Hospital for Federal soldiers, Nashville, Tennessee, 1864.

ABOVE LEFT: Guns outside the Capitol, Nashville, in 1864.

ABOVE: The Federal outer line, Nashville, on 16 December, 1864.

LEFT: A fortified railroad bridge, across the Cumberland river, Nashville, in 1864.

on 19 November 1864, with Hood's troops reaching Columbia on the Duck river on 27 November. Union troops at Pulaski withdrew to Nashville, while more Union troops headed for Columbia to dig in before Hood arrived. As Hood approached and tried to get round Columbia, the Union troops, under Schofield, also pulled back.

Hood advanced towards Franklin, where he encountered more Union troops. There was a sharp fight, which inflicted relatively heavy casualties on the Confederates, and Hood's army was significantly weakened by this engagement and the arrival of more Union troops. Grant, Lincoln and others now realized there was a golden opportunity to destroy the Confederate Army of Tennessee, but Thomas was not yet ready to launch a major offensive. He was waiting for additional cavalry and Grant eventually lost his patience and decided to replace Thomas with Schofield on 9 December. As it was, the Battle of Nashville took place between 15 and 16 December 1864. Union troops amounted to some 55,000, with Hood's strength a little under 38,000.

ABOVE: Fort Pulaski, Georgia.

RIGHT: Atlanta, the Confederate lines, 1864.

THE CIVIL WAR

The Union army advanced to push the Confederates out of their entrenchments around Nashville, pushing them back a short distance on the first day. Fighting continued into 16 December and this time determined attacks broke through and made Hood's positions untenable, completing the disintegration of Hood's army. Thomas, still in charge, as Schofield had not yet replaced him, took over 13,000 Confederate prisoners. Hood resigned his command but was ordered to Texas to organize troops. He would eventually turn himself into the Union army in late May 1865.

Sherman's famous March to the Sea

LEFT: Sherman's men rip up railroad tracks in Georgia, 1864.

BELOW LEFT: Sherman's men in Atlanta.

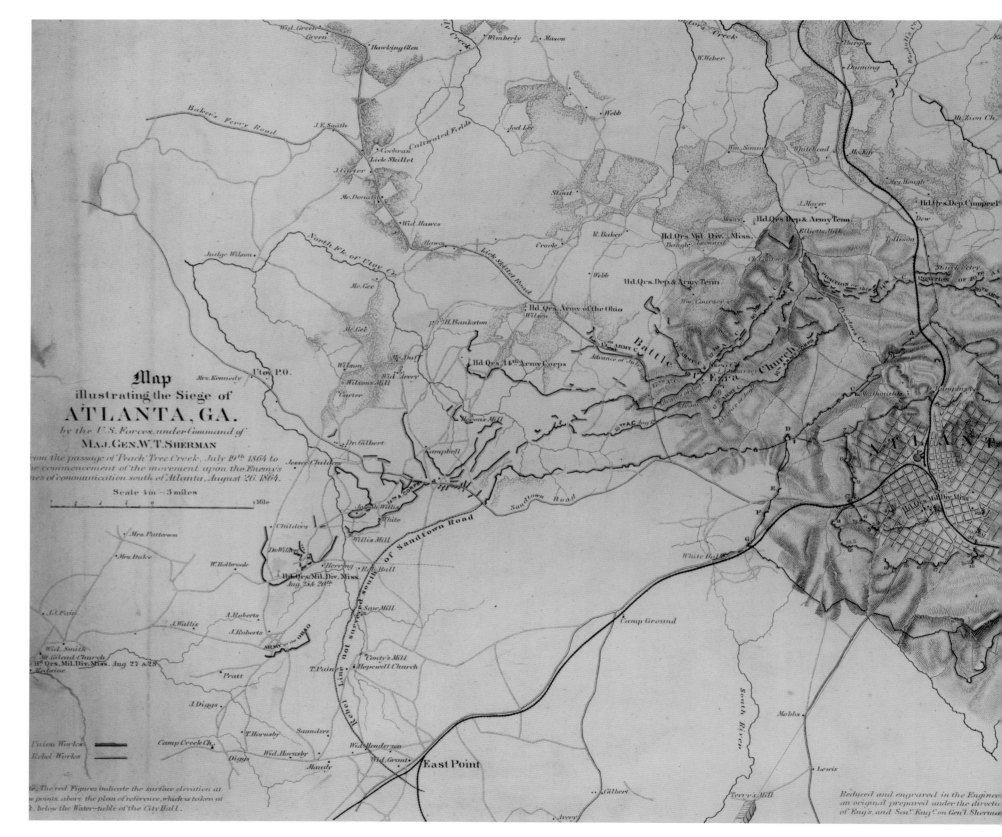

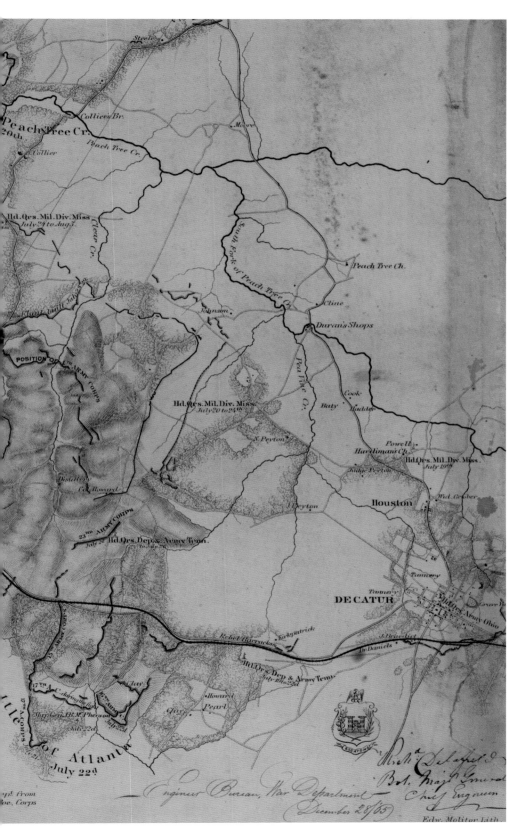

FAR LEFT: Map illustrating the Siege of Atlanta, Georgia, 26 August 1864.

LEFT: Lt. General William J. Hardee.

occurred in the autumn of 1864 when, with around 60,000 troops at his disposal, he marched from Kingston to Savannah, a distance of over 300 miles (480km), between 12 November and 22 December 1864. During the march he destroyed factories, stores, mills, in fact anything he thought would support the Confederate armies. His troops occupied Savannah on 22 December, where he received reinforcements, men being now available following the destruction of Hood's army. Sherman's march caused a great outcry at the time and has been much criticized over the years for its destructive nature. Between 14 and 16 November Sherman's army destroyed much of Atlanta, leaving the city in flames.

The Confederates were almost completely powerless to stop Sherman, and all that could be scraped together were around 10,000 regular troops to protect Savannah. In fact Sherman did not meet with any real opposition until he was almost at Savannah, where the Confederates had thrown up some fortifications, but were quickly carried at bayonet point. The Confederates in Savannah, under General

THE ROAD TO VICTORY

RIGHT: Ruined houses in Savannah, Georgia.

BELOW: Sherman's troops removing ammunition from Fort McAllister, near Savannah.

BELOW RIGHT: A Confederate gun at Fort McAllister.

Hardee, abandoned the city on 20 December, and having reached his goal, Sherman was then ordered to turn north to cut off Confederate troops from joining Lee's Army of Northern Virginia. Consequently, Sherman's troops entered Columbia, South Carolina, on 17 February 1865.

Facing Sherman in this region was a Confederate army under Beauregard. He had nowhere near enough men to deal with Sherman, forcing him to abandon Charleston and Wilmington. Beauregard seemed to have lost the ability to fight and Lee replaced him with General Joseph E. Johnston on 23 February. The Confederates tried to harass Sherman as best they could, but they were fighting a losing battle. There were fights, but most of them were merely large skirmishes.

Sherman arrived in Fayetteville on 11 March and established communication with Union forces operating further north.

Johnston was still determined to stop Sherman, attempting to oppose him 4 miles (6km) from Bentonville on 19 March. The initial Confederate attack was successful, but by the afternoon Sherman had significantly reinforced his front line and Johnston realized that the game was up and that he faced being surrounded. Johnston had been able to amass only some 14,000 men and while casualties were relatively even, over 600 Confederates were taken prisoner.

Sherman reached Goldsboro on 23 March, by which stage his army had marched 425 miles (684km) from Savannah, over the worst possible terrain, and had crossed five rivers.

Things had not gone well for the Confederacy in the North and Richmond had been imperilled. Back in May 1864 Grant had begun his offensive in the Wilderness and Union troops had moved up the James river. By 9 May Union troops were heading towards Petersburg, though Richmond was the ultimate goal. What had

ABOVE LEFT and *ABOVE:*
Confederate fortifications, Atlanta.

LEFT: Ruins of a rail depot left by Sherman's men.

RIGHT: Ruins of Charleston, South Carolina.

BELOW RIGHT: Houses along Charleston's Battery, damaged by shell-fire.

OPPOSITE ABOVE LEFT: Ruins of the North-Eastern Railroad depot, Charleston.

OPPOSITE ABOVE RIGHT: Ruins of church and buildings in Charleston.

OPPOSITE BELOW LEFT: Confederate Artillery at Charleston.

OPPOSITE BELOW RIGHT: The New Capitol at Columbia, South Carolina, in ruins.

really changed the course of the campaign in Virginia was the realization on Grant's part that he could not dislodge Lee from his entrenchments to the north of the James river. Grant decided he would have to try to get behind Lee and cut him off from his supplies, and proposed to move to the south side of the James river.

There was a vicious fight at Piedmont, near Staunton, on 5 June 1864 and another at Lynchburg between 17 and 18 June. What has always remained an unanswered question is why Lee did not stop, or at least challenge Grant, when he crossed the Chickahominy and James rivers. Some believe this failure was even worse than that of Gettysburg.

By early June Union forces were testing the defences at Petersburg, which had been hastily manned. After Richmond, Petersburg was the most important Confederate centre in Virginia. Beauregard commanded the Confederates and realized he had insufficient troops. Petersburg, just 23 miles (37km) from Richmond, had a population of

18,000, and was built on the south bank of the Appomattox river. The problem for the Confederates was that Grant's troops were north of the James river, and were presenting as much of a threat to Lee as the Union troops, that were threatening Petersburg, were to Beauregard.

Grant believed that Petersburg could be taken relatively easily and ordered troops to move up from Bermuda Hundred to Petersburg on 15 June, with orders to take Petersburg as quickly as possible. The troops, under General Smith, amounted to some 16,000 and Beauregard had just 5,400 men. For some bizarre reason Smith failed to capitalize on the opportunity, which meant that Grant had to lay siege to Petersburg from June 1864 until April 1865.

By 18 June Lee was ordering troops to Petersburg, the vanguard of his army adding 25,000 men to the defence, and by lunchtime Lee was there himself. In the attacks on Petersburg, between 15 and 18 June, Union losses amounted to some 10,000 men, but Lee was now dug in along a 25-mile (40-km)

ABOVE: Libby Prison, Richmond, Virginia, 1865.

ABOVE RIGHT: A crippled locomotive of the Richmond & Petersburg Railroad, destroyed by the Federal Army in 1865.

RIGHT: Richmond in ruins, 1865.

OPPOSITE: View of the James river and Kanawah Canal near the Haxall Flour Mills, with the ruins of the Galego Mills beyond, 1865.

front, covering Richmond and Petersburg from White Oak Swamp to Jerusalem Plank Road.

The actual assaults on the Confederate lines took place on 17 and 18 June, primarily by troops under the command of General Burnside. Central to this engagement was what became known as the Battle of the Crater. Union engineers had excavated a tunnel over 500ft (150m) long, extending directly under the Confederate fortifications. Some 8,000lb (3630kg) of gunpowder was dragged into the tunnel and was detonated at 1645 on 30 July 1864, causing a huge blast and blowing a vast hole, some 30ft deep, 60ft wide and 170ft long (9 x 18 x 50m) in the

THE CIVIL WAR

Confederate defences. Union troops were then pushed into the crater to take advantage of the Confederate shock, resulting in costly hand-to-hand fighting and Union losses that amounted to nearly 4,000 men. The finger of blame was pointed at Burnside, who was removed from his command.

On 18 August 1864 Union troops tried to destroy the Weldon Railroad, which led to a violent confrontation costing the lives of over 4,000 Union troops. The railroad was again attacked from 22 to 24 August, leading to a further engagement on 25 August.

The final offensive of the Confederates at Petersburg took place on 25 March 1865, when Lee ordered an attack on Fort Stedman on Hare's Hill and 10,000 Confederates, under Major General Gordon, stormed the fort and captured several batteries of artillery. Union troops were ordered to counter-attack, and led by the 200th Pennsylvania, they took the fort in 20 minutes at a cost of 122 men. Other Pennsylvanian units overran the captured batteries and 1,600 Confederates were captured.

It had become increasingly obvious that there was nothing Lee could do to stop Grant's army from linking up with Sherman's forces. There was another disaster at Five Forks, Virginia, on 1 April, when Sheridan destroyed a Confederate

OPPOSITE: Converted ferryboat on the James river.

BELOW LEFT: The monitor USS Onondaga on the James river in 1864, with soldiers rowing ashore in the foreground.

Defiance: Inviting a Shot Before Petersburg, 1864
Winslow Homer (1836–1910).
Oil on canvas.
The Detroit Institute of Arts,
USA/Founders Society purchase and
Dexter M. Ferry Jr. fund.

force under Major General Pickett. Sheridan also destroyed railroads, mills and factories around Charlottesville and then, at the head of 10,000 cavalry, headed for the White House, having taken 4,500 prisoners.

On the morning of 2 April 1865 Lee was sure he had to abandon Petersburg and retreat towards Richmond, it being only a matter of time before Grant overran the Petersburg defences.

Grant and Lee had already met while serving in Mexico. Early in March 1865 Lee approached Grant with a view to ending the war. But Grant and Lee were military men and not politicians and it would be left to others to make the decisions. On 7 April 1865 Grant invited the surrender of Lee's army. He had reached Farmville and wrote to Lee: 'The result of last week must convince you of the hopelessness of further resistance on the part of the Army of Northern Virginia in this struggle. I feel that it is so, and regard it as my duty to shift from myself the responsibility of any further effusion of blood, by asking of you the surrender of that portion of the Confederate army known as the Army of Northern Virginia.'

Lee's reply was not exactly as Grant had

OPPOSITE ABOVE LEFT and BELOW: Fortifications, Petersburg, Virginia.

OPPOSITE ABOVE RIGHT: Camp of the 13th New York Artillery, Petersburg.

ABOVE LEFT: Camp of Companies, Petersburg.

ABOVE: The medical supply boat, Planter, on the Appomattox river.

LEFT: Appomattox Courthouse.

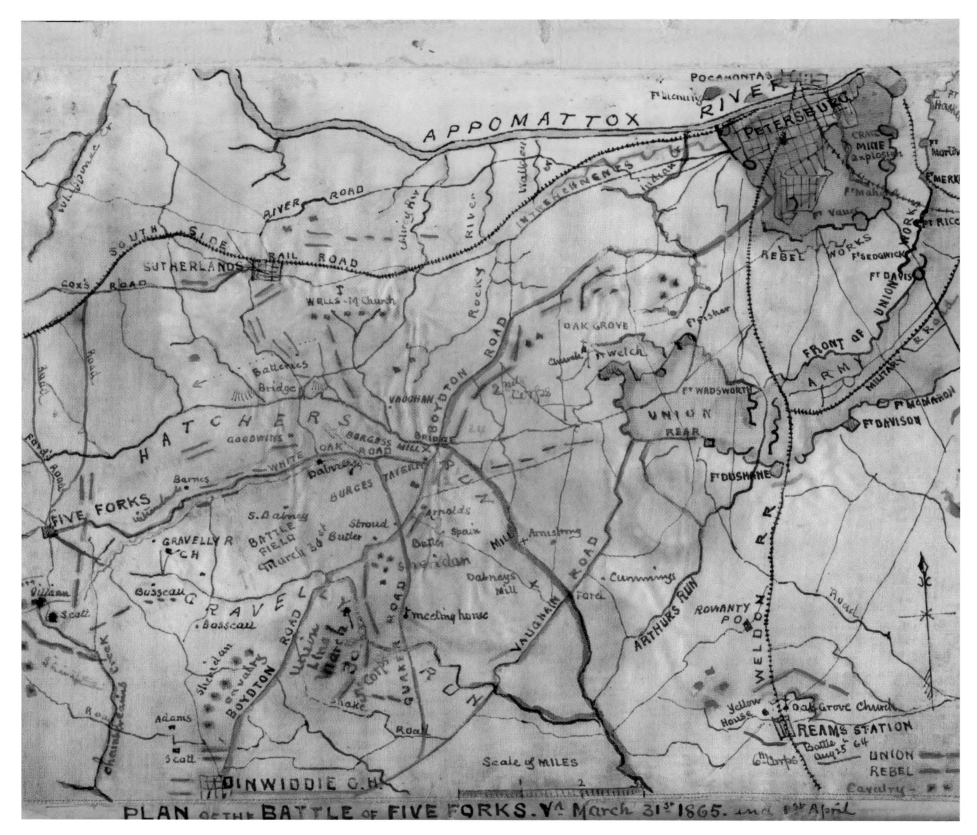

hoped. Lee did not regard the situation as hopeless, but he was unwilling for more blood to be uselessly shed and wanted to know what the conditions of surrender might be.

Grant informed Lee that terms could be discussed, yet Lee was still not sure if the situation was as desperate as it seemed. By 8 April, while Lee's army was resting to the east of Appomattox Courthouse, Lee proposed to see if Grant was blocking

escape routes, and if he was, then there would be no option but to surrender.

Custer's cavalry made a dash to destroy the railroad to the west of Appomattox Station, but was attacked by Confederate troops at dawn the following day. As he fell back, however, more Union troops moved up in support. Lee and Grant determined to meet and discuss the terms of surrender. To this end, a Union officer would lead Lee to the village of Appomattox Courthouse,

where he would meet with Grant in a house owned by Wilmer McLean. Grant arrived shortly after 1300 on 9 April. His terms were: 'The officers and men surrendered to be paroled and disqualified from taking up arms again until properly exchanged and all arms, ammunition, and supplies to be delivered up as captured property.'

Lee knew he had no choice. The two men talked for a while after signing, and at 1600 Lee left, the two meeting again the

OPPOSITE: Plan of the Battle of Five Forks, 31 March–1 April 1865.

ABOVE: Major General George G. Meade and his staff.

THE CIVIL WAR

following morning. The official surrender of the troops took place on 12 April, with Confederate regiments arriving at a field near Appomattox Courthouse, where they stacked their arms and colours. Some 26,018 men surrendered and were then paroled.

Meanwhile, Sherman was pushing towards Raleigh in North Carolina, when he heard about the surrender at Appomattox. It was 13 April and the inhabitants of Raleigh ran towards his troops carrying white flags. Elements of his cavalry were at Greensboro and others near Columbus and Macon, Georgia, and Sherman was intending to cut off General Johnston's retreat.

The following day, the Union received a note from Johnston to Sherman, proposing a temporary truce. They agreed to meet near Durham Station on 17 April but, as Sherman was about to get on the train, he received word that Lincoln had been assassinated. Sherman went ahead with the meeting and learned that Johnston was prepared to surrender his troops once he had received permission from the Confederate President Davis. They met again the following day, when haggling took place.

Under the terms of Lincoln's Proclamation of Amnesty of 8 December 1863, any Confederate below the rank of colonel would be given an immediate pardon. Grant had extended that pardon to all officers, including Lee himself, and Johnston was keen for a similar bargain to be struck. One of the sticking points, however, was John C. Breckinridge, who was the Confederate Secretary of War, but had also been the Vice President of the United States. The only advice Sherman could give Johnston where Breckinridge was concerned was that he should leave the country and never return.

An outline agreement was ready for presentation to Washington on 18 April. Washington wanted terms no better nor worse than the ones Lee had been forced to sign. Johnston had no choice and the terms were signed on 26 April.

The total number of men involved in Johnston's agreement was 89,270. There

were, of course, isolated commands that did not surrender at this stage. In fact there was another major engagement in Texas as late as mid-May 1865. The battle took place between 12 and 13 May and ended in a victory for the Confederacy. As the former Confederate President Jefferson Davis wrote in his memoirs: 'Though very small in comparison to its great battles, [Palmito Ranch] deserves notice as having closed the long struggle as it opened, with a Confederate victory.'

OPPOSITE: Soldiers on the banks of the Appomattox river at Johnson's Mill.

BELOW: High bridge on the South Side Railroad crossing the Appomattox river near Farmville.

221

THE ROAD TO VICTORY

CHAPTER TEN
THE CASUALTIES OF WAR

RIGHT: The assassination of President Lincoln, at Ford's Theatre, Washington D.C. on 14 April 1865.

BELOW: President Lincoln.

BELOW RIGHT: Actor John Wilkes Booth, Lincoln's assassin.

When Abraham Lincoln was inaugurated for the second time on 4 March 1865 the war was nearly over. The conflict had actually cost far more than would have been needed to buy the freedom of each individual slave in the South. Only five days after the surrender of Lee's Army of Northern Virginia, Abraham Lincoln, like thousands of other Americans during the American Civil War, met a violent end at the hands of a man with a gun.

Lincoln had been due to attend a performance of *Our American Cousin* at Ford's Theatre in Washington on the night of 14 April 1865. He arrived with his wife and guests at 2030, but at 2200, halfway through the final act, an assassin slipped into the corridor behind the presidential box, opened the door, and shot Lincoln through the head. Lincoln was mortally wounded and died of his injuries at 0722 the next day.

The killer was a Southerner, an actor by the name of John Wilkes Booth. Lincoln represented everything Booth hated most, and he took his chance to strike at the man he saw as responsible for the downfall of the South. Booth was tracked down to a barn in Virginia, which was set on fire. Someone saw him moving within the building, and shot at him, and Booth staggered out and died.

For a country such as the United States, barely a century old and still expanding, the Civil War had involved vast numbers of men. In July 1861 the Union army had been able to muster some 187,000 men, compared with the Confederacy's 112,000. By 1865 the Union army had increased to nearly a million (up to 50,000 in the U.S. Navy) and the Confederate armies could boast 450,000 men.

Battlefield casualties had been severe, with major battles involving up to 100,000 Union troops and 60,000 Confederates. In all, some 110,000 Union troops were killed in the field or died of their wounds, compared with around 90,000 Confederate casualties.

Disease took even more soldiers: an estimated 360,000 Union and 260,000 Confederates died of malaria, typhoid and dysentery, or as a direct result of their wounds. It has been estimated that the American Civil War cost the United States $20 billion, a huge sum of money, but the cost in human lives was, of course, far more devastating and affected families in all sections of American society. Lincoln's own wife lost three brothers fighting for the Confederacy, and his sister-in-law was the widow of the Confederate officer, Benjamin Helm, who died at Chickamauga.

Family links such as these prompted

THE CIVIL WAR

Old Hill Burial Ground, a Civil War cemetery.

THE CASUALTIES OF WAR

heated debates and accusations after the war, while associates of Lincoln's assassin, Booth, had death penalties imposed. Indeed some of them were implicated in a failed plot to assassinate the Secretary of State, William Seward, to coincide with the murder of Abraham Lincoln.

Further accusations were levelled at John C. Breckinridge, who had been President James Buchanan's vice president, in that he had been part of a pre-war Southern conspiracy to derail the Union. Even Lincoln was accused of having pro-slavery leanings, having come from Kentucky, a slave state, though any suggestions that Lincoln may have favoured the South were dispelled when he was murdered.

Though some suspected a major Southern conspiracy behind the assassination of Lincoln, in fact there was none. None of the Confederate leaders had any idea that Booth had been planning to assassinate the president. Had the killing taken place much earlier, before Antietam and the subsequent Emancipation Proclamation, the resolve of the South may have been called into question.

On paper, at least, the war should never

ABOVE: The 3rd Connecticut Infantry at Camp Douglas, 1861.

RIGHT: James Buchanan.

FAR RIGHT: The 93rd New York Infantry at Antietam.

have lasted so long, nor should there have been so many casualties. In many respects the style of government in the South had been instrumental in allowing the Confederates to be more flexible and to reward their more superior commanders with swift promotion. By the end of the war the South had 17 lieutenant generals and eight full generals, giving them far better chains of command.

The North, on the other hand, frequently allowed overbearing and overcautious politicians to interfere with the running of the Union army, while the seemingly overwhelming strength of the Army of the Potomac was held back by a string of poor appointments. McClellan led the army twice and Washington tried to make it a force to be reckoned with, using McDowell, Pope, Burnside, Hooker and Meade to achieve this aim. At various times the vast army moved at a snail's pace, barely able to defend itself, while at others its strength was dissipated as it blundered forward with reckless abandon.

Militarily, the principal difference between the North and the South was the way in which the armies had been led. To begin with, perhaps, the Southern troops had had the edge, but as the war progressed

Going Home
Julian Scott (1846–1901), 1887.
Oil on canvas.
Private collection.

THE CASUALTIES OF WAR

with deprivation and danger on the battlefield as long as they had faith in their officers. Here the Confederates scored well: often up against a numerically superior foe, they fought the larger Union armies to a standstill.

As the war progressed, the Southern troops had to accept that their own homes and land were under occupation or threat by Union troops. It is testament to their resolve that they stayed with the main field armies and did not desert to protect their own property. Both sides were facing what appeared to be an indifferent civilian population and even worse were the men who had avoided conscription and were making fat profits from the war behind the lines. In fact, profits could be made on both sides of the front line and even at the height of the Union blockades, only half the blockade-runners were intercepted by the Union navy. This meant that expensive imported products, if they could be obtained, would find a ready market anywhere a speculator chose to offer them.

There are many issues to ponder when the American Civil War is examined in detail. First and foremost there was the balance of manpower and resources, where the Union always had a distinct advantage. Nevertheless, it has been asked on many occasions why it took four years to crush the Confederacy, when it was so woefully weaker than the

ABOVE: Depot of the 17th New York Artillery.

RIGHT: Bodies at the Gaines' Mill battle site awaiting burial.

the Union troops were better trained and began to equal them on the battlefield. On both sides, officer casualties were disproportionately large, in that aggressive commanders at company, regimental level, and above had to lead their men from the front.

Despite the huge numbers under arms, many of the troops in the early years were volunteers and thousands sought to evade conscription, while thousands more fled when faced with a determined enemy. The penalty for desertion, for both Union and Confederate soldiers, was death, but this rarely needed to be carried out. This was because men were prepared to suffer within the bosom of their regiment, rather than face life outside it, and were willing to cope

THE CIVIL WAR

Union. The first answer relates directly to the use of available resources, in that to begin with, the Union was simply wasteful, while the South put its manpower and resources to direct and practical use. The second is the leadership of the military. Again, as we have seen, the Union armies fluctuated from being timid to aggressive, according to the commander who was in charge at the time.

The South certainly had the upper hand, at least until Antietam, and probably beyond. It so nearly won the key battle at Gettysburg, which would have led to the destruction of the main Union force of the Army of the Potomac, and would have left much of the North, including Washington, at its mercy. Considering the relatively short distance between Richmond and Washington, it is also a wonder why neither capital fell sooner; Richmond, however, did ultimately fall towards the end of the war. In fact the majority of the battles were fought over a relatively small area of the United States, principally in the East, and Virginia can claim the dubious honour of hosting more battles during the Civil War than any other state.

Had key Union commanders, such as Grant, Sheridan and Sherman, come to the

LEFT: Federal dead at Gettysburg.

BELOW LEFT: Flag of the 37th Pennsylvania Infantry.

BELOW: Soldiers' graves at City Point, Virginia.

Howard's Grove Hospital, near Richmond, Virginia
American School (19th century).
Chicago Historical Museum, Chicago.

THE CASUALTIES OF WAR

The Jefferson Memorial, Washington, D.C.

fore earlier and had been given full rein to prosecute their versions of total war, even Lee could not have stood in their way in achieving a quick and effective victory.

For both sides, the key to victory had always been the use of strategy and communications, coupled with effective logistics. The Confederacy quite rightly adopted a defensive strategy, fighting on its own ground so that communications and resupply were the more effective. For the Union it was an offensive war, in that it was necessary to forge a way into the South, seize land and population centres and keep them. The South, after all, was hostile territory, so as more of it began to fall, more Union troops could be diverted to the mundane task of occupation.

Their individual strategical approaches reflect the difference in aspirations of the Confederacy and the Union. At no time did the Confederacy seriously wish to impose its government on the North, but as far as the Union was concerned, it was the exact opposite; it did wish to impose its will on the South and this was what dictated the offensive and defensive strategies used by the two sides.

Once Union troops had begun to occupy the South, the Confederacy had to rely on mobile armies, which could cut into the occupation zones and seize weapons, ammunition, food and horses from the invading Union troops. This strategy worked extremely well for a long time and Confederate soldiers were able to rely on the Union army to supply them, often with food and goods they had not seen for months, as a result of their ill-defended supply centres.

The Confederates did, of course, do far more than simply counter-attack the weak points of the Union front line. In 1863 Lee launched a massive raid into the North, with the objective of harassing Northern civilians and, of course, drawing out an ill-prepared Union army that could be defeated in a decisive manner on the battlefield.

Both sides should have realized that the way in which the war was being fought had direct parallels with the American Revolution, when it was the British who

THE CIVIL WAR

seized the ground and established garrisons, only to find themselves vulnerable because they had not cornered Washington's army and destroyed it. For several months this was exactly the predicament in which the Union army found itself, while facing an aggressive and elusive Robert E. Lee.

Both the Confederates and the Union were obsessed with taking the other's capitals and defending their own. False alarms at various times led to thousands of Union troops being diverted to holding the approaches to Washington, while on other occasions, vast Union armies that could have done far more harm to the Confederacy, fruitlessly sat around Richmond or battered themselves to a standstill against the capital's defences.

The South was ultimately doomed, not when Richmond came under threat, but when the Union forces gained control of the Mississippi Valley. Sherman's 2,000-mile (3220-km) rampage through Georgia and the Carolinas wrecked the South's infrastructure and proved once and for all that the Confederate armies were incapable of stopping a determined Union force.

Towards the end of the war there were fewer set-piece battles, it being more a question of the two armies being in continual contact with one another. They would clash when one army advanced too quickly or when one was too tardy in retreat. This remorseless form of warfare, with no peace, no time for rest or recuperation, could only have one victor: the Union. It is true to say that the South never did receive a mortal blow, but died the death of a thousand cuts.

To reiterate, the American Civil War was fought not to end slavery but to preserve the Union. Rightly or wrongly, the Southern states, seizing on a technicality in the constitutional agreements, effectively withdrew from the Union, and everything that happened from this point on was either in defence of their right to secede or to prevent the Union from making them change their minds.

But perhaps this was not the whole story. As Lincoln himself confessed at his second inaugural address: 'All knew that this interest [Southern slavery] was, somehow, the cause of this war.'

If this is what Lincoln really believed, then we return to the question, why did he not bow to the abolitionists earlier? Possibly the preservation of the Union just tipped the balance; Lincoln had written to Frederick Douglass that he would emancipate all, some or none of the slaves to achieve this aim.

In the post-war period, many commentators and historians tried to get to the root of the causes and effects of the American Civil War. To some, the war was a matter of economics, the North wishing to bring the South fully into its economic empire and crush, once and for all, any notion of independence, while others claim the war had been totally avoidable. Some thought the North, and Lincoln in particular, had given in too easily to the demands of abolitionist extremists and that it was the inherent threat of emancipation that had forced the secession of the South. But other kinds of extremists had been active in the South; they had a vested interest in preserving slavery, and by pressing their case they had forced the South to take the ultimate step.

The time following the Civil War was known as the Reconstruction Period, when infrastructure was rebuilt, the North and South were redefined, and efforts were made to bring a greater degree of homogeneity to the United States.

The South, the war's battlefield and the centre of slavery, struggled to come to terms with defeat and suffered even more during the post-war years. Economically, it fell even further behind the North and the disparity in wealth and population increased. The South fell prey to speculators able to make rich profits at the expense of Southern landowners. The cotton industry did recover, but this time it was operated using paid workers. Post-war, Great Britain, for example, was now importing far more Southern cotton than it had before the conflict.

As for the former slaves, their long journey towards truly equal rights would have to continue until it became an unstoppable force 90 years later. As for Lincoln, he had once said that there could be no regrets about the war, in that it would provide the necessary conditions for 'A just, and a lasting peace.'

BELOW: Army of the Potomac horse artillery.

Lincoln's Drive through Richmond
Dennis Malone Carter (1827–81), 1866.
Oil on canvas.
Chicago Historical Museum, Chicago.

TIME LINE OF THE CIVIL WAR

DATE	EVENT
1860	
November 6	Abraham Lincoln elected president
December 20	South Carolina secedes from the Union, followed two months later by other states.
1861	
February 9	Jefferson Davis becomes the first and only President of the Confederate States of America
March 4	Lincoln sworn in as 16th President of the United States
April 12	Confederates, under Beauregard, open fire on Fort Sumter at Charleston, South Carolina
April 15	Lincoln issues a proclamation calling for 75,000 volunteers
April 17	Virginia secedes from the Union, followed by three other states, making an 11-state Confederacy
April 19	Blockade proclamation issued by Lincoln
April 20	Robert E. Lee resigns his command in the United States Army
July 4	Congress authorizes a call for half a million volunteers
July 21	Union forces, under McDowell, defeated at Bull Run
July 27	McClellan replaces McDowell
November 1	McClellan becomes general-in-chief of Union forces after the resignation of Winfield Scott
November 8	Two Confederate officials are seized en route to Great Britain by the Union navy
1862	
February 6	Grant captures Fort Henry in Tennessee
March 8–9	The Confederate ironclad *Merrimac* sinks two Union warships, then fights the *Monitor*
April 6–7	Confederates attack Grant at Shiloh on the Tennessee river
April 24	Union ships under Farragut take New Orleans
May 31	Battle of Seven Pines, where Joseph E. Johnston is badly wounded when he nearly defeats McClellan's army
June 1	Robert E. Lee takes over from Johnston and renames the force the Army of Northern Virginia
June 25–July 1	Lee attacks McClellan near Richmond during the Seven Days' Battles. McClellan retreats towards Washington
July 11	Henry Halleck becomes general-in-chief of the Union army
August 29–30	Union army, under Pope, defeated by Jackson and Longstreet at the Second Battle of Bull Run
September 4–9	Lee invades the North, pursued by McClellan's Union army
September 17	Battle of Antietam. Both sides are badly mauled. Lee withdraws to Virginia
September 22	Preliminary Emancipation Proclamation issued by Lincoln
November 7	McClellan replaced by Burnside as commander of the Army of the Potomac
December 13	Burnside decisively defeated at Fredericksburg, Virginia, 1863
1863	
January 1	Lincoln issues the final Emancipation Proclamation
January 29	Grant assumes command of the Army of the West
March 3	U.S. Congress authorizes conscription
May 1–4	Hooker is decisively defeated by Lee at the Battle of Chancellorsville. Stonewall Jackson is mortally wounded

THE CIVIL WAR

June 3 — Lee invades the North, heading into Pennsylvania

June 28 — George Meade replaces Hooker as commander of the Army of the Potomac

July 1–3 — Lee is defeated at the Battle of Gettysburg

July 4 — Vicksburg – the last Confederate stronghold on the Mississippi – falls to Grant and the Confederacy is now split in two

July 13–16 — Draft riots in New York

July 18 — 54th Massachusetts, under Shaw, fails in its assault against Fort Wagner, South Carolina

August 21 — Quantrill's raiders murder the inhabitants of Lawrence, Kansas

September 19–20 — Bragg's Confederate Army of Tennessee defeats General Rosecrans at Chickamauga

October 16 — Grant given command of all operations in the West

November 19 — Lincoln gives his famous Gettysburg Address

November 23–25 — Grant defeats Bragg at Chattanooga

1864
March 9 — Grant assumes command of all armies of the Union.

Sherman takes Grant's old job as commander in the West

May 5–6 — Battle of the Wilderness

May 8–12 — Battle of Spotsylvania

June 1–3 — Battle of Cold Harbor

June 15 — Union troops miss a chance to capture Petersburg

July 20 — Sherman defeats Hood at Atlanta

August 29 — Former General McClellan becomes the Democratic nominee for president

September 2 — Atlanta is captured by Sherman

October 19 — Sheridan defeats Early's Confederates in the Shenandoah Valley

November 8 — Lincoln is re-elected president

November 15 — Sherman begins his March to the Sea

December 15–16 — Hood is defeated at the Battle of Nashville

December 21 — Sherman reached Savannah in Georgia.

1865
January 31 — Thirteenth amendment approved to abolish slavery

February 3 — Peace conference between Lincoln and Confederate vice president fails at Hampton

Roads, Virginia

March 4 — Lincoln inaugurated as president

March 25 — Lee's last offensive is defeated after four hours at Petersburg

April 2 — Grant pushes through Lee's defensive lines at Petersburg. Richmond is evacuated as Union troops enter

April 4 — Lincoln tours Richmond

April 9 — Lee surrenders his army to Grant at Appomattox Courthouse, Virginia

April 10 — Major victory celebrations in Washington

April 14 — Lincoln shot in a Washington theatre

April 15 — Lincoln dies and Andrew Johnson becomes president

April 18 — Confederate General Johnston surrenders to Sherman in North Carolina

April 19 — Lincoln's funeral procession

April 26 — Lincoln's assassin, Booth, is shot and dies in Virginia

May 23–24 — Victory parade held in Washington

December 6 — Thirteenth Amendment approved by Congress. It is ratified and slavery is formally abolished

The Field Hospital
Eastman Johnson (1824–1906), 1867.
Oil on paperboard.
Private collection.

EXAMPLES OF UNION (FEDERAL) UNIFORMS

Ulysses S. Grant in his general's uniform

5th New York Volunteers

Indiana Regiment

39th New York Voluntry Infantry Regiment

U.S. Marine Corps

Iron Brigade of the U.S.

THE CIVIL WAR

Trooper. U.S. Volunteer Cavalry

U.S. Corps of Engineers

U.S. Naval Officer

Union Army Staff Officer

U.S. Sharpshooter

U.S. Colored Infantry

243

EXAMPLES OF CONFEDERATE UNIFORMS

Robert E. Lee in his general's uniform

Marines

Trooper, Stuart's Cavalry Corps.

Infantry Soldier

Privateer and Blockade Runner

Virginia Cavalry

244

THE CIVIL WAR

Louisiana Tigers

Georgia Infantry

Navy

South Carolina Regiment

Engineer

4th Alabama Regiment.

245

**Captain Hickenlooper's Battery in the
Hornet's Nest at the Battle of Shiloh,
April 1862**
T.C. Lindsay (1845–1907).
Lithograph.
Private collection.

INDEX

INDEX

INDEX

INDEX

AKNOWLEDGEMENTS

Pages 8–9 Museum of Fine Arts, Boston, Massachusetts/The Bridgeman Art Library: Page 10 (both) Art Directors & Trip Photo Library/Brian Vikander: Page 11 Library of Congress, Washington, DC: Page 12 (all) Library of Congress, Washington, DC: Page 13 (all) Library of Congress, Washington, DC: Pages 14–15 Library of Congress, Washington, DC/The Bridgeman Art Library: Page 16 (all) Library of Congress, Washington, DC: Page 17 (both) Library of Congress, Washington, DC: Pages 18–19 © Private collection/Peter Newark American Pictures/The Bridgeman Art Library: Pages 20 and 21 Art Directors & Trip Photo Library/Earl Young/John Wallace: Page 22 Art Directors & Trip Photo Library/Jeff Greenberg: Page 23 (both) Library of Congress, Washington, DC: Page 24 Art Directors & Trip Photo Library/Brian Vikander: Page 25 Art Directors & Trip Photo Library/Jeff Greenberg: Page 26 Art Directors & Trip Photo Library/Earl Young: Page 27 Library of Congress, Washington, DC: Page 28 Library of Congress, Washington, DC: Page 29 (both) Library of Congress, Washington, DC: Page 30 Library of Congress, Washington, DC: Page 31 (both) Library of Congress, Washington, DC: Page 32 (both) Library of Congress, Washington, DC: Page 33 Library of Congress, Washington, DC: Page 34 (all) Library of Congress, Washington, DC: Page 35 Library of Congress, Washington, DC: Page 36 (all) Library of Congress, Washington, DC: Page 37 (both) Library of Congress, Washington, DC: Page 38 (all) Library of Congress, Washington, DC: Page 39 (both) Library of Congress, Washington, DC: Page 40 (both) Library of Congress, Washington, DC: Page 41 (all) Library of Congress, Washington, DC: Page 42 (both) Library of Congress, Washington, DC: Page 43 (all) Library of Congress, Washington, DC: Page 44 (both) Library of Congress, Washington, DC: Page 45 (all) Library of Congress, Washington, DC: Page 46 (all) Library of Congress, Washington, DC: Page 47 Art Directors & Trip Photo Library/Brian Vikander: Page 48 Library of Congress, Washington, DC: Page 49 (all) Library of Congress, Washington, DC: Pages 50–51 © Collection of the New York Historical Society/The Bridgeman Art Library: Pages 53–53 © Private collection/Peter Newark Military Pictures/The Bridgeman Art Library: Pages 54–55 © Collection of the New York Historical Society/The Bridgeman Art Library: Page 56 (all) Library of Congress, Washington, DC: Page 57 (all) Library of Congress, Washington, DC: Pages 58–59 © Chicago Historical Museum/The Bridgeman Art Library: Page 60 (both) Library of Congress, Washington, DC: Page 61 (all) Library of Congress, Washington, DC: Pages 62–63 © Private collection/The Bridgeman Art Library: Pages 64–65 Art Directors & Trip Photo Library: Page 65 (right) Library of Congress, Washington, DC: Pages 66–67 © Chicago Historical Museum/The Bridgeman Art Library: Page 68 Library of Congress, Washington, DC: Page 69 Library of Congress, Washington, DC: Page 70 (all) Library of Congress, Washington, DC: Page 71 (all) Library of Congress, Washington, DC: Pages 72–73 © Private collection/Peter Newark Military Pictures/The Bridgeman Art Library: Page 74 (all) Library of Congress, Washington, DC: Page 75 Library of Congress, Washington, DC: Pages 76–77 © Private collection/Peter Newark Military Pictures/The Bridgeman Art Library: Page 78 Library of Congress, Washington, DC: Page 79 Library of Congress, Washington, DC: Page 80 (all) Library of Congress, Washington, DC: Page 81 (all) Library of Congress, Washington, DC: Pages 82–83 Art Directors & Trip Photo Library: Page 83 (right) Library of Congress, Washington, DC: Page 84 (left) Art Directors & Trip Photo Library/Brian Vikander: Page 84 (centre) Art Directors & Trip Photo Library/Jerry Dennis: Page 85 (both) Library of Congress, Washington, DC: Page 86 (all) Library of Congress, Washington, DC: Page 87 (both) Library of Congress, Washington, DC: Page 88 (both) Library of Congress, Washington, DC: Page 89 left (both) Library of Congress, Washington, DC: Page 89 (right) Art Directors & Trip Photo Library/Jeff Greenberg: Pages 90–91 © Newberry Library, Chicago, Illinois/The Bridgeman Art Library: Pages 92–93 (all) Library of Congress, Washington, DC: Page 94 Art Directors & Trip Photo Library/Jeff Greenberg: Page 95 (all) Library of Congress, Washington, DC: Page 96 (all) Library of Congress, Washington, DC: Page 97 (left) Art Directors & Trip Photo Library/Jerry Dennis: Page 97 (right) Library of Congress, Washington, DC: Pages 98–99 (all) Library of Congress, Washington, DC: Pages 100–101 © David David Gallery, Philadelphia, Pennsylvania/The Bridgeman Art Library: Pages 102–103 (both) Library of Congress, Washington, DC: Page 104 (left) Library of Congress, Washington, DC: Page 104 (centre) Art Directors & Trip Photo Library/Jeff Greenberg: Page 105 (right) Library of Congress, Washington, DC: Pages 106–107 © Chicago Historical Museum/The Bridgeman Art Library: Page 108 (top) Library of Congress, Washington, DC: Page 108 (below) Art Directors & Trip Photo Library/Jeff Greenberg: Page 109 (left) Art Directors & Trip Photo Library/Jeff Greenberg: Page 109 (right) Library of Congress, Washington, DC: Page 110 © Delaware Art Museum, Wilmington/Bequest of Jessie Harrington/The Bridgeman Art Library: Page 111 © Private collection/The Bridgeman Art Library: Page 112 (all) Library of Congress, Washington, DC: Page 113 (both) Library of Congress, Washington, DC: Page 114 Library of Congress, Washington, DC: Page 115 (all) Library of Congress, Washington, DC: Pages 116–117 © Collection of the New York Historical Society/The Bridgeman Art Library: Page 118 (both) Library of Congress, Washington, DC: Page 119 (both) Library of Congress, Washington, DC: Pages 120–121 © Private collection/Christie's Images/The Bridgeman Art Library: Page 122 Library of Congress, Washington, DC: Page 123 Library of Congress, Washington, DC: Page 124 © Collection of the New York Historical Society/The Bridgeman Art Library: Page 125 (right) © Private collection/Christie's Images/The Bridgeman Art Library: Page 126 Library of Congress, Washington, DC: Page 127 (all) Library of Congress, Washington, DC: Pages 128–129 © David David Gallery, Philadelphia, Pennsylvania/The Bridgeman Art Library: Page 130 (all) Library of Congress, Washington, DC: Page 131 (both) Library of Congress, Washington, DC: Page 132 © Private collection/The Bridgeman Art Library: Page 133 © Indianapolis Museum of Art/The Bridgeman Art Library: Page 134 (all) Library of Congress, Washington, DC: Page 135 (all) Library of Congress, Washington, DC: Page 136 (both) Library of Congress, Washington, DC: Page 137 (all) Library of Congress, Washington, DC: Pages 138–139 © Private collection/Peter Newark Military Pictures/The Bridgeman Art Library: Page 140 Art Directors & Trip Photo Library/Jeff Greenberg: Page 141 (right) Library of Congress, Washington, DC: Page 142 (both) Library of Congress, Washington, DC: Page 143 Library of Congress, Washington, DC: Page 144 (both) Library of Congress, Washington, DC: Page 145 (all) Library of Congress, Washington, DC: Page 146 Library of Congress, Washington, DC: Page 147 Art Directors & Trip Photo Library/Douglas Houghton: Page 148 © Philadelphia Museum of Art, Pennsylvania/The Bridgeman Art Library: Pages 148–149 Atwater Kent Museum of Philadelphia/Courtesy of the Historical Society of Pennsylvania Collection/The Bridgeman Art Library: Page 150 (both) Library of Congress, Washington, DC: Page 151 (all) Library of Congress, Washington, DC: Pages 152–153 © Private collection/The Bridgeman Art Library: Page 154 Library of Congress, Washington, DC: Page 155 (both) Library of Congress, Washington, DC: Pages 156–157 © Chicago Historical Museum/The Bridgeman Art Library: Page 158 Art Directors & Trip Photo Library/Jeff Greenberg: Page 159 Library of Congress, Washington, DC: Page 160 (all) Library of Congress, Washington, DC: Page 161 Library of Congress, Washington, DC: Pages 162–163 (all) Library of Congress, Washington, DC: Page 164 (both) Library of Congress, Washington, DC: Page 165 Library of Congress, Washington, DC: Page 166 (both) Library of Congress, Washington, DC: Page 167 (all) Library of Congress, Washington, DC: Page 168 Library of Congress, Washington, DC: Page 169 (all) Library of Congress, Washington, DC: Page 170 (both) Library of Congress, Washington, DC: Page 171 (both) Library of Congress, Washington, DC: Page 172 (both) Library of Congress, Washington, DC: Page 173 Library of Congress, Washington, DC: Pages 174–175 © Chicago Historical Museum/The Bridgeman Art Library: Page 176 Library of Congress, Washington, DC: Page 177 Library of Congress, Washington, DC: Page 178 (all) Library of Congress, Washington, DC: Page 179 Library of Congress, Washington, DC: Page 180 (both) Library of Congress, Washington, DC: Page 181 Library of Congress, Washington, DC: Page 182 (both) Library of Congress, Washington, DC: Page 183 Library of Congress, Washington, DC: Page 184 Library of Congress, Washington, DC: Page 185 Library of Congress, Washington, DC: Pages 186–187 © Atwater Kent Museum of Philadelphia/Courtesy of the Historical Society of Pennsylvania Collection/The Bridgeman Art Library: Page 188 (all) Library of Congress, Washington, DC: Page 189 Library of Congress, Washington, DC: Page 190 (all) Library of Congress, Washington, DC: Page 191 Library of Congress, Washington, DC: Pages 192–193 © Smithsonian Institution, Washington DC/The Bridgeman Art Library: Page 194 © Chicago Historical Museum/The Bridgeman Art Library: Page 195 Library of Congress, Washington, DC: Page 196 (all) Library of Congress, Washington, DC: Page 197 (all) Library of Congress, Washington, DC: Page 198 (both) Library of Congress, Washington, DC: Page 199 Art Directors & Trip Photo Library/Keith Cardwell: Page 200 Library of Congress, Washington, DC: Page 201 (all) Library of Congress, Washington, DC: Page 202 (both) Library of Congress, Washington, DC: Page 203 (both) Library of Congress, Washington, DC: Page 204–205 (both) Library of Congress, Washington, DC: Page 206 (all) Library of Congress, Washington, DC: Page 207 (all) Library of Congress, Washington, DC: Page 208 (both) Library of Congress, Washington, DC: Page 209 (all) Library of Congress, Washington, DC: Page 210 (all) Library of Congress, Washington, DC: Page 211 Library of Congress, Washington, DC: Page 212 Library of Congress, Washington, DC: Page 213 Library of Congress, Washington, DC: Pages 214–215 © The Detroit Institute of Arts/Founders Society purchase and Dexter M. Ferry Jr. fund/The Bridgeman Art Library: Page 216 (all) Library of Congress, Washington, DC: Page 217 (all) Library of Congress, Washington, DC: Page 218 Library of Congress, Washington, DC: Page 219 Library of Congress, Washington, DC: Page 220 Library of Congress, Washington, DC: Page 221 Library of Congress, Washington, DC: Page 222 Art Directors & Trip Photo Library/Jeff Greenberg: Page 223 Art Directors & Trip Photo Library/Jeff Greenberg: Page 224 (all) Library of Congress, Washington, DC: Page 225 Art Directors & Trip Photo Library/Richard Surman: Page 226 Library of Congress, Washington, DC: Page 227 (both) Library of Congress, Washington, DC: Pages 228–229 © Private collection/Christie's Images/The Bridgeman Art Library: Page 230 (both) Library of Congress, Washington, DC: Page 231 (all) Library of Congress, Washington, DC: Pages 232–233 © Chicago Historical Museum/The Bridgeman Art Library: Page 234 Art Directors & Trip Photo Library/J. R. Livermore: Page 235 Library of Congress, Washington, DC: Pages 236–237 © Chicago Historical Museum/The Bridgeman Art Library: Pages 240–241 © Private collection/Gift of Maxim Karolik for the M. & M. Karolik Collection of American Paintings (1815–65)/The Bridgeman Art Library: Pages 242–245 Artwork Mike Codd: Pages 246–247 © Private collection/Peter Newark's Military Pictures/The Bridgeman Art Library.

BIBLIOGRAPHY

Catton, Bruce. *The Centennial History of the Civil War*, Doubleday, 1962.

Coddington, Edwin. *The Gettysburg Campaign*, Scribners, 1984.

Donald, David. *Divided We Fought*, Macmillan, 1952

Foote, Shelby. *The Civil War: A Narrative* (3 volumes), Random House, 1986

Grant, Ulysses S. *Personal Memoirs of U.S. Grant*, Webster, 1886

Hansen, Harry. *The Civil War.* Mentor Books, 1961

Leckie, Robert. *None Died in Vain.* HarperCollins, 1990

Lee, Ulysses. *The Employment of Negro Troops*, Government Printing Office, 1966

Mitchell, Joseph. *Decisive Battles of the Civil War*, Putnam, 1955

Sutherland, Jonathan. *Battles of the American Civil War*, Airlife, 2002

Sutherland, Jonathan. *Commanders and Heroes of the American Civil War*, Airlife, 2002

Tucker, Glenn. *High Tide at Gettysburg*, Smithmark, 1994